DOVER · THRIFT · EDITIONS

Little Orphant Annie and Other Poems

JAMES WHITCOMB RILEY

DOVER PUBLICATIONS, INC.
New York

DOVER THRIFT EDITIONS

General Editor: Stanley Appelbaum
Editor of This Volume: Candace Ward

Copyright

Published in Canada by General Publishing Company, Ltd., 30 Lesmill Road, Don Mills, Toronto, Ontario.
Published in the United Kingdom by Constable and Company, Ltd., 3 The Lanchesters, 162–164 Fulham Palace Road, London W6 9ER.

Bibliographical Note

This Dover edition, first published in 1994, is a new selection of 24 poems reprinted from standard texts. The Note and alphabetical list of titles and first lines have been specially prepared for this edition.

Library of Congress Cataloging-in-Publication Data

Manufactured in the United States of America
Dover Publications, Inc., 31 East 2nd Street, Mineola, N.Y. 11501

Note

JAMES WHITCOMB RILEY (1849–1916) was born in Greenfield, Indiana. Riley showed little interest in his formal public education, but he spent many hours at the popular spots in Greenfield—the courthouse, the cobbler's shop and wherever else people gathered—listening to the local stories and lore, soaking up the dialect and mannerisms of rural Indiana. Though primarily remembered for his poetry, Riley was also an accomplished musician, actor and painter. Before turning his talents to journalism, Riley traveled throughout Indiana, first painting advertisements on barns and fences, then working as a musician and actor for a traveling medicine show.

By 1877, Riley was the local editor for the Anderson *Democrat*. While there he achieved much notoriety for publishing *Leonainie*, a poem supposedly by Edgar Allan Poe, but actually written by Riley himself. Though a successful hoax, the stunt cost Riley his job and caused him embarrassment the rest of his life. He then went to work for the Indianapolis *Journal*, where he stayed from 1877–1885. There Riley contributed a series of poems in the Hoosier dialect, writing under the pen name Benjamin F. Johnson. In 1883 a collection of these poems was published in *"The Old Swimmin'-Hole" and 'Leven More Poems*. Riley's poetry was so successful that it brought him greater financial success than any other American poet had enjoyed to that date. Lecture tours increased his popularity and allowed him to display his skills as an actor and humorist. Today Riley is remembered as a poet who preserved both a time and place in American letters through the use of Hoosier dialect and homely themes.

The poems in this edition were revised and edited by Riley over the years, and many appeared in more than one volume of his poetry, and in different forms. (See the Bibliographical Note on page ii for the volume in which the poems first appeared.) The text of the poems presented here reflect the author's final revisions.

Contents

Little Orphant Annie

INSCRIBED
WITH ALL FAITH AND AFFECTION

To all the little children:—The happy ones; and sad ones;
The sober and the silent ones; the boisterous and glad ones;
The good ones—Yes, the good ones, too; and all the lovely bad ones.

Little Orphant Annie's come to our house to stay,
An' wash the cups an' saucers up, an' brush the crumbs away,
An' shoo the chickens off the porch, an' dust the hearth, an' sweep,
An' make the fire, an' bake the bread, an' earn her board-an'-keep;
An' all us other childern, when the supper-things is done,
We set around the kitchen fire an' has the mostest fun
A-list'nin' to the witch-tales 'at Annie tells about,
An' the Gobble-uns 'at gits you
Ef you
Don't
Watch
Out!

Wunst they wuz a little boy wouldn't say his prayers,—
An' when he went to bed at night, away up-stairs,
His Mammy heerd him holler, an' his Daddy heerd him bawl,
An' when they turn't the kivvers down, he wuzn't there at all!
An' they seeked him in the rafter-room, an' cubby-hole, an' press,
An' seeked him up the chimbly-flue, an' ever'-wheres, I guess;
But all they ever found wuz thist his pants an' roundabout:—
An' the Gobble-uns 'll git you
Ef you
Don't
Watch
Out!

An' one time a little girl 'ud allus laugh an' grin,
An' make fun of ever' one, an' all her blood-an'-kin;
An' wunst, when they was "company," an' ole folks wuz there,

She mocked 'em an' shocked 'em, an' said she didn't care!
An' thist as she kicked her heels, an' turn't to run an' hide,
They wuz two great big Black Things a-standin' by her side,
An' they snatched her through the ceilin' 'fore she knowed what
she's about!
An' the Gobble-uns 'll git you
Ef you
Don't
Watch
Out!

An' little Orphant Annie says, when the blaze is blue,
An' the lamp-wick sputters, an' the wind goes *woo-oo!*
An' you hear the crickets quit, an' the moon is gray,
An' the lightnin'-bugs in dew is all squenched away,—
You better mind yer parunts, an' yer teachurs fond an' dear,
An' churish them 'at loves you, an' dry the orphant's tear,
An' he'p the pore an' needy ones 'at clusters all about,
Er the Gobble-uns 'll git you
Ef you
Don't
Watch
Out!

An Old Sweetheart of Mine

An old sweetheart of mine!—Is this her presence here with me,
Or but a vain creation of a lover's memory?
A fair, illusive vision that would vanish into air
Dared I even touch the silence with the whisper of a prayer?

Nay, let me then believe in all the blended false and true—
The semblance of the *old* love and the substance of the *new*,—
The *then* of changeless sunny days—the *now* of shower and
shine—
But Love forever smiling—as that old sweetheart of mine.

This ever-restful sense of *home*, though shouts ring in the hall.—
The easy chair—the old book-shelves and prints along the wall;
The rare *Habanas* in their box, or gaunt church-warden-stem
That often wags, above the jar, derisively at them.

As one who cons at evening o'er an album, all alone,
And muses on the faces of the friends that he has known,
So I turn the leaves of Fancy, till, in shadowy design,
I find the smiling features of an old sweetheart of mine.

The lamplight seems to glimmer with a flicker of surprise,
As I turn it low—to rest me of the dazzle in my eyes,
And light my pipe in silence, save a sigh that seems to yoke
Its fate with my tobacco and to vanish with the smoke.

'Tis a *fragrant* retrospection,—for the loving thoughts that start
Into being are like perfume from the blossom of the heart;
And to dream the old dreams over is a luxury divine—
When my truant fancies wander with that old sweetheart of mine.

Though I hear beneath my study, like a fluttering of wings,
The voices of my children and the mother as she sings—
I feel no twinge of conscience to deny me any theme
When Care has cast her anchor in the harbor of a dream—

In fact, to speak in earnest, I believe it adds a charm
To spice the good a trifle with a little dust of harm,—
For I find an extra flavor in Memory's mellow wine
That makes me drink the deeper to that old sweetheart of mine.

O Childhood-days enchanted! O the magic of the Spring!—
With all green boughs to blossom white, and all bluebirds to sing!
When all the air, to toss and quaff, made life a jubilee
And changed the children's song and laugh to shrieks of ecstasy.

With eyes half closed in clouds that ooze from lips that taste, as well,
The peppermint and cinnamon, I hear the old School bell,
And from "Recess" romp in again from "Blackman's" broken line,
To smile, behind my "lesson," at that old sweetheart of mine.

A face of lily beauty, with a form of airy grace,
Floats out of my tobacco as the Genii from the vase;
And I thrill beneath the glances of a pair of azure eyes
As glowing as the summer and as tender as the skies.

I can see the pink sunbonnet and the little checkered dress
She wore when first I kissed her and she answered the caress
With the written declaration that, "as surely as the vine
Grew 'round the stump," she loved me—that old sweetheart of
mine.

Again I made her presents, in a really helpless way,—
The big "Rhode Island Greening"—I was hungry, too, that day!—
But I follow her from Spelling, with her hand behind her—so—
And I slip the apple in it—and the Teacher doesn't know!

I give my *treasures* to her—all,—my pencil—blue-and-red;—
And, if little girls played marbles, *mine* should all be *hers*, instead!
But *she* gave me her *photograph*, and printed "Ever Thine"
Across the back—in blue-and-red—that old sweetheart of mine!

And again I feel the pressure of her slender little hand,
As we used to talk together of the future we had planned,—
When I should be a poet, and with nothing else to do
But write the tender verses that she set the music to . . .

When we should live together in a cozy little cot
Hid in a nest of roses, with a fairy garden-spot,
Where the vines were ever fruited, and the weather ever fine,
And the birds were ever singing for that old sweetheart of mine.

When I should be her lover forever and a day,
And she my faithful sweetheart till the golden hair was gray;
And we should be so happy that when either's lips were dumb
They would not smile in Heaven till the other's kiss had come.

But, ah! my dream is broken by a step upon the stair,
And the door is softly opened, and—my wife is standing there:
Yet with eagerness and rapture all my visions I resign;—
To greet the *living* presence of that old sweetheart of mine.

The Old Swimmin'-Hole

Oh! the old swimmin'-hole! whare the crick so still and deep
Looked like a baby-river that was laying half asleep,
And the gurgle of the worter round the drift jest below
Sounded like the laugh of something we onc't ust to know
Before we could remember anything but the eyes
Of the angels lookin' out as we left Paradise;
But the merry days of youth is beyond our controle,
And it's hard to part ferever with the old swimmin'-hole.

Oh! the old swimmin'-hole! In the happy days of yore,
When I ust to lean above it on the old sickamore,
Oh! it showed me a face in its warm sunny tide
That gazed back at me so gay and glorified,
It made me love myself, as I leaped to caress
My shadder smilin' up at me with sich tenderness.
But them days is past and gone, and old Time's tuck his toll
From the old man come back to the old swimmin'-hole.

Oh! the old swimmin'-hole! In the long, lazy days
When the humdrum of school made so many run-a-ways,
How plesant was the jurney down the old dusty lane,
Whare the tracks of our bare feet was all printed so plane
You could tell by the dent of the heel and the sole
They was lots o' fun on hands at the old swimmin'-hole.
But the lost joys is past! Let your tears in sorrow roll
Like the rain that ust to dapple up the old swimmin'-hole.

Thare the bullrushes growed, and the cattails so tall,
And the sunshine and shadder fell over it all;
And it mottled the worter with amber and gold
Tel the glad lilies rocked in the ripples that rolled;
And the snake-feeder's four gauzy wings fluttered by
Like the ghost of a daisy dropped out of the sky,
Or a wownded apple-blossom in the breeze's controle
As it cut acrost some orchurd to'rds the old swimmin'-hole.

Oh! the old swimmin'-hole! When I last saw the place,
The scenes was all changed, like the change in my face;
The bridge of the railroad now crosses the spot
Whare the old divin'-log lays sunk and fergot.
And I stray down the banks whare the trees ust to be—
But never again will theyr shade shelter me!
And I wish in my sorrow I could strip to the soul,
And dive off in my grave like the old swimmin'-hole.

A Letter to a Friend

The past is like a story
  I have listened to in dreams
That vanished in the glory
  Of the Morning's early gleams;
And—at my shadow glancing—
  I feel a loss of strength,
As the Day of Life advancing
  Leaves it shorn of half its length.

But it's all in vain to worry
  At the rapid race of Time—
And he flies in such a flurry
  When I trip him with a rhyme,
I'll bother him no longer
  Than to thank you for the thought
That "my fame is growing stronger
  As you really think it ought."

And though I fall below it,
  I might know as much of mirth
To live and die a poet
  Of unacknowledged worth;
For Fame is but a vagrant—
  Though a loyal one and brave,
And his laurels ne'er so fragrant
  As when scattered o'er the grave.

Fame

I

Once, in a dream, I saw a man
  With haggard face and tangled hair,
  And eyes that nursed as wild a care
As gaunt Starvation ever can;
And in his hand he held a wand
  Whose magic touch gave life and thought
  Unto a form his fancy wrought
And robed with coloring so grand,
  It seemed the reflex of some child
  Of Heaven, fair and undefiled—
  A face of purity and love—
  To woo him into worlds above:
And as I gazed with dazzled eyes,
  A gleaming smile lit up his lips
  As his bright soul from its eclipse
Went flashing into Paradise.
Then tardy Fame came through the door
And found a picture—nothing more.

II

And once I saw a man, alone,
  In abject poverty, with hand
Uplifted o'er a block of stone
  That took a shape at his command
And smiled upon him, fair and good—
A perfect work of womanhood,
Save that the eyes might never weep,
Nor weary hands be crossed in sleep,
Nor hair that fell from crown to wrist,
Be brushed away, caressed and kissed.
And as in awe I gazed on her,
  I saw the sculptor's chisel fall—

I saw him sink, without a moan,
Sink lifeless at the feet of stone,
And lie there like a worshiper.
Fame crossed the threshold of the hall,
And found a statue—that was all.

III

And once I saw a man who drew
A gloom about him like a cloak,
And wandered aimlessly. The few
Who spoke of him at all but spoke
Disparagingly of a mind
The Fates had faultily designed:
Too indolent for modern times—
Too fanciful, and full of whims—
For, talking to himself in rhymes,
And scrawling never-heard-of hymns,
The idle life to which he clung
Was worthless as the songs he sung!
I saw him, in my vision, filled
With rapture o'er a spray of bloom
The wind threw in his lonely room;
And of the sweet perfume it spilled
He drank to drunkenness, and flung
His long hair back, and laughed and sung
And clapped his hands as children do
At fairy tales they listen to,
While from his flying quill there dripped
Such music on his manuscript
That he who listens to the words
May close his eyes and dream the birds
Are twittering on every hand
A language he can understand.
He journeyed on through life, unknown,
Without one friend to call his own;
He tired. No kindly hand to press
The cooling touch of tenderness
Upon his burning brow, nor lift

To his parched lips God's freest gift—
No sympathetic sob or sigh
Of trembling lips—no sorrowing eye
Looked out through tears to see him die.
And Fame her greenest laurels brought
To crown a head that heeded not.

And this is Fame! A thing, indeed,
That only comes when least the need:
The wisest minds of every age
The book of life from page to page
Have searched in vain; each lesson conned
Will promise it the page beyond—
Until the last, when dusk of night
Falls over it, and reason's light
Is smothered by that unknown friend
Who signs his *nom de plume*, The End.

A Child's Home—Long Ago

READ AT AN OLD SETTLERS' MEETING AT OAKLAND, INDIANA, AUGUST 3, 1878.

The terse old maxim of the poet's pen,
"What constitutes a state? High-minded men,"
Holds such a wealth of truth, when one reflects,
It seems more like a sermon than a text.
Yet looking dimly backward o'er the years
Where first the face of progress, through our tears,
Smiles on us, where within the forest gloom
The bud of Indiana bursts in bloom;
We can but see, from Lake of Michigan,
To where Ohio rolls, the work of man—

From where our eastern boundary-line is pressed,
To where the Wabash revels on the west;
A broad expanse of fair and fertile land,
Like some rich landscape, from a master's hand,
That in its rustic frame, we well might call
The fairest picture on Columbia's wall—
A picture now—a masterpiece divine,
That, ere the artist's hand in its design
Had traced this loveliness, was but a blot
Of ugly pigment on a barren spot—
A blur of color on a hueless ground
Where scarce a hint of beauty could be found.
But patiently the hand of labor wrought,
And from each touch new inspiration caught;
Toiled on through disadvantages untold,
And at each onward step found firmer hold,
And obstacles that threatened long delay
He climbed above and went upon his way,
Until at last, exulting, he could see
The sweet reward of patient industry;
And beauties he had hardly dared to dream,
In hill and vale, and cliff and winding stream,
Spread out before his vision, till the soul
Within him seemed to leap beyond control,
And hover over lands the genii made
Of sifted sunshine and of dew-washed shade.

And who, indeed, that loves his native state,
Has not a heart to throb and palpitate
With ecstasy, as o'er her wintry past,
He sees the sun of summer dawn at last,
And catches, through the misty shower of light,
Dim glimpses of the orchards' bloom of white,
And fields beyond where, waving empty sleeves,
The "scarecrow" beckons to the feathered thieves
That perch, and perk their nimble heads away,
And flit away with harsh, discordant cry,
Or shading with his hand, his dazzled eyes,
Looks out across the deadened paradise,
Where wild flowers blossom, and the ivy clings,

And from the ruined oak the grape-vine swings,
While high above upon the leafless tree
The red-head drummer beats his reveille,
And, like an army thronging at the sound,
The soldier corn-stalks on their battleground
March on to harvest victories, and flaunt
Their banners o'er the battlements of want!

And musing thus to-day, the pioneer
Whose brawny arm has grubbed a pathway here,
Stands, haply; with his vision backward turned
To where the log-heap of the past was burned,
And sees again, as in some shadowy dream,
The wild deer bending o'er the hidden stream,
Or sniffing, with his antlers lifted high,
The gawky crane, as he comes trailing by,
And drops in shallow tides below to wade
On tilting legs through dusky depths of shade,
While just across the glossy otter slips
Like some wet shadow 'neath the ripple's lips
As, drifting from the thicket-hid bayou,
The wild duck paddles past his rendezvous,
And overhead the beech and sycamore,
That lean their giant forms from either shore,
Clasp hands and bow their heads, as though to bless
In whispered prayer the sleeping wilderness.
A scene of such magnificent expanse
Of nameless grandeur that the utterance
Of even feathered orators is faint.
For here the dove's most melancholy plaint
Invokes no echo, and the killdeer's call
Swoons in the murmur of the waterfall
That, faint and far away and undefined,
Falls like a ghost of sound upon the mind.
The voice of nature's very self drops low,
As though she whispered of the long ago,
When down the wandering stream the rude canoe
Of some lone trapper glided into view,
And loitered down the watery path that led
Through forest depths that only knew the tread

Of savage beasts; and wild barbarians
That skulked about with blood upon their hands
And murder in their hearts. The light of day
Might barely pierce the gloominess that lay
Like some dark pall across the water's face,
And folded all the land in its embrace;
The panther's whimper, and the bear's low growl—
The snake's sharp rattle, and the wolf's wild howl;
The owl's grim chuckle, as it rose and fell
In alternation with the Indian's yell,
Made fitting prelude for the gory plays
That were enacted in the early days.

But fancy, soaring o'er the storm of grief
Like that lone bird that brought the olive leaf,
Brings only peace—an amulet whose spell
Works stranger marvels than the tongue can tell—
For o'er the vision, like a mirage, falls
The old log cabin with its dingy walls,
And crippled chimney with its crutch-like prop
Beneath a sagging shoulder at the top:
The coonskin battened fast on either side—
The wisps of leaf-tobacco—"cut-and-dried";
The yellow strands of quartered apples, hung
In rich festoons that tangle in among
The morning-glory vines that clamber o'er
The little clapboard roof above the door:
The old well-sweep that drops a courtesy
To every thirsting soul so graciously,
The stranger, as he drains the dripping gourd,
Intuitively murmurs, "Thank the Lord!"
Again through mists of memory arise
The simple scenes of home before the eyes:—
The happy mother, humming, with her wheel,
The dear old melodies that used to steal
So drowsily upon the summer air,
The house-dog hid his bone, forgot his care,
And nestled at her feet, to dream, perchance,
Some cooling dream of winter-time romance:
The square of sunshine through the open door

That notched its edge across the puncheon floor,
And made a golden coverlet whereon
The god of slumber had a picture drawn
Of Babyhood, in all the loveliness
Of dimpled cheek and limb and linsey dress:
The bough-filled fireplace, and the mantel wide,
Its fire-scorched ankles stretched on either side,
Where, perched upon its shoulders 'neath the joist,
The old clock hiccoughed, harsh and husky-voiced,
And snarled the premonition, dire and dread,
When it should hammer Time upon the head:
Tomatoes, red and yellow, in a row,
Preserved not then for diet, but for show,—
Like rare and precious jewels in the rough
Whose worth was not appraised at half enough:
The jars of jelly, with their dusty tops;
The bunch of pennyroyal; the cordial drops;
The flask of camphor, and the vial of squills,
The box of buttons, garden-seeds, and pills;
And, ending all the mantel's bric-à-brac,
The old, time-honored "Family Almanack."
And Memory, with a mother's touch of love,
Climbs with us to the dusky loft above,
Where drowsily we trail our fingers in
The mealy treasures of the harvest bin;
And, feeling with our hands the open track,
We pat the bag of barley on the back;
And, groping onward through the mellow gloom,
We catch the hidden apple's faint perfume,
And, mingling with it, fragrant hints of pear
And musky melon ripening somewhere.
Again we stretch our limbs upon the bed
Where first our simple childish prayers were said;
And while, without, the gallant cricket trills
A challenge to the solemn whippoorwills,
And, filing on the chorus with his glee,
The katydid whets all the harmony
To feather-edge of incoherent song,
We drop asleep, and peacefully along
The current of our dreams we glide away

To the dim harbor of another day,
Where brown toil waits for us, and where labor stands
To welcome us with rough and horny hands.

And who will mock the rude, unpolished ways
That swayed us in the good old-fashioned days
When labor wore the badge of manhood, set
Upon his tawny brow in pearls of sweat?
Who dares to-day to turn a scornful eye
On labor in his swarthy majesty?
Or wreathe about his lips the sneer of pride
Where brawny toil stands towering at his side?
By industry alone we gauge the worth
Of all the richer nations of the earth;
And side by side with honesty and toil
Prosperity walks round the furrowed soil
That belts the world, and o'er the ocean ledge
Tilts up the horn of plenty on its edge.
'Tis not the subject fawning to the king,
'Tis not the citizen, low cowering
Before the throne of state.—'Twas God's intent
Each man should be a king—a president;
And while through human veins the blood of pride
Shall ebb and flow in Labor's rolling tide,
The brow of toil shall wear the diadem,
And justice gleaming there, the central gem,
Shall radiate the time when we shall see
Each man rewarded as his works shall be.
Thank God for this bright promise! Lift the voice
Till all the waiting multitudes rejoice;
Reach out across the sea and clap your hands
Till voices waken out of foreign lands
To join the song, while listening Heaven waits
To roll an answering anthem through the gates.

August

A day of torpor in the sullen heat
   Of Summer's passion: In the sluggish stream
The panting cattle lave their lazy feet,
   With drowsy eyes, and dream.

Long since the winds have died, and in the sky
   There lives no cloud to hint of Nature's grief;
The sun glares ever like an evil eye,
   And withers flower and leaf.

Upon the gleaming harvest-field remote
   The thresher lies deserted, like some old
Dismantled galleon that hangs afloat
   Upon a sea of gold.

The yearning cry of some bewildered bird
   Above an empty nest, and truant boys
Along the river's shady margin heard—
   A harmony of noise—

A melody of wrangling voices blent
   With liquid laughter, and with rippling calls
Of piping lips and thrilling echoes sent
   To mimic waterfalls.

And through the hazy veil the atmosphere
   Has draped about the gleaming face of Day,
The sifted glances of the sun appear
   In splinterings of spray.

The dusty highway, like a cloud of dawn,
   Trails o'er the hillside, and the passer-by,
A tired ghost in misty shroud, toils on
   His journey to the sky.

And down across the valley's drooping sweep
   Withdrawn to farthest limit of the glade,
The forest stands in silence, drinking deep
   Its purple wine of shade.

The gossamer floats up on phantom wing;
   The sailor-vision voyages the skies
And carries into chaos everything
   That freights the weary eyes:

Till, throbbing on and on, the pulse of heat
   Increases—reaches—passes fever's height,
And Day slinks into slumber, cool and sweet,
   Within the arms of Night.

In the Dark

O in the depths of midnight
   What fancies haunt the brain!
When even the sigh of the sleeper
   Sounds like a sob of pain.

A sense of awe and of wonder
   I may never well define,—
For the thoughts that come in the shadows
   Never come in the shine.

The old clock down in the parlor
   Like a sleepless mourner grieves,
And the seconds drip in the silence
   As the rain drips from the eaves.

And I think of the hands that signal
   The hours there in the gloom,
And wonder what angel watchers
   Wait in the darkened room.

And I think of the smiling faces
   That used to watch and wait,

Till the click of the clock was answered
By the click of the opening gate.—

They are not there now in the evening—
Morning or noon—not there;
Yet I know that they keep their vigil,
And wait for me Somewhere.

A Peace-Hymn of the Republic

LOUISVILLE, KENTUCKY, SEPTEMBER 12, 1895: TWENTY-NINTH ENCAMPMENT, G.A.R.[1]

There's a Voice across the Nation like a mighty ocean-hail,
Borne up from out the Southward as the seas before the gale;
Its breath is in the streaming Flag and in the flying sail—
As we go sailing on.

'Tis a Voice that we remember—ere its summons soothed as now—
When it rang in battle-challenge, and we answered vow with vow,—
With roar of gun and hiss of sword and crash of prow and prow,
As we went sailing on.

Our hope sank, even as we saw the sun sink faint and far,—
The Ship of State went groping through the blinding smoke of War—
Through blackest midnight lurching, all uncheered of moon or star,
Yet sailing—sailing on.

As One who spake the dead awake, with life-blood leaping warm—
Who walked the troubled waters, all unscathed, in mortal form,—
We felt our Pilot's presence with His hand upon the storm,
As we went sailing on.

1. G.A.R.] Grand Army of the Republic.

O Voice of passion lulled to peace, this dawning of To-day—
O Voices twain now blent as one, ye sing all fears away,
Since foe and foe are friends, and lo! the Lord, as glad as they.—
He sends us sailing on.

The Old Home by the Mill

This is "The Old Home by the Mill"—fer we still call it so,
Although the *old mill*, roof and sill, is all gone long ago,
The old home, though, and the old folks—the old spring, and a few
Old cattails, weeds and hartychokes, is left to welcome you!

Here, Marg'et!—fetch the man a *tin* to drink out of! Our spring
Keeps kindo'-sorto' cavin' in, but don't "*taste*" anything!
She's kindo' *agin'*, Marg'et is—"the *old* process"—like me,
All ham-stringed up with rhumatiz, and on in seventy-three.

Jest me and Marg'et lives alone here—like in long ago;
The childern all putt off and gone, and married, don't you know?
One's millin' 'way out West somewhare; two other miller-boys
In Minnyopolis they air; and one's in Illinoise.

The *oldest* gyrl—the first that went—married and died right here;
The next lives in Winn's Settlement—fer purt' nigh thirty year!
And youngest one—was allus fer the old home here—but no!—
Her man turns in and he packs *her* 'way off to Idyho!

I don't miss them like *Marg'et* does—'cause I got *her*, you see;
And when she pines for them—that's cause *she's* only jest got *me!*
I laugh, and joke her 'bout it all.—But talkin' sense, I'll say,
When she was tuk so bad last Fall, I laughed then t'other way!

I hain't so favor'ble impressed 'bout *dyin'*; but ef I
Found I was only second-best when *us two* come to die,
I'd 'dopt the "new process," in full, ef *Marg'et* died, you see,—
I'd jest crawl in my grave and pull the green grass over me!

The Dead Lover

Time is so long when a man is dead!
  Some one sews; and the room is made
Very clean; and the light is shed
  Soft through the window-shade.

Yesterday I thought: "I know
  Just how the bells will sound, and how
The friends will talk, and the sermon go,
  And the hearse-horse bow and bow!"

This is to-day; and I have no thing
  To think of—nothing whatever to do
But to hear the throb of the pulse of a wing
  That wants to fly back to you.

A Vision of Summer

Twas a marvelous vision of Summer.—
  That morning the dawn was late,
And came, like a long dream-ridden guest,
  Through the gold of the Eastern gate.

Languid it came, and halting
  As one that yawned, half roused,
With lifted arms and indolent lids
  And eyes that drowsed and drowsed.

A glimmering haze hung over
  The face of the smiling air;
And the green of the trees and the blue of the leas
  And the skies gleamed everywhere.

And the dewdrops' dazzling jewels,
  In garlands and diadems,
Lightened and twinkled and glanced and shot
  At the glints of a thousand gems:

Emeralds of dew on the grasses;
  The rose with rubies set;
On the lily, diamonds; and amethysts
  Pale on the violet.

And there were the pinks of the fuchsias,
  And the peony's crimson hue,
The lavender of the hollyhocks,
  And the morning-glory's blue:

The purple of the pansy bloom,
  And the passionate flush of the face
Of the velvet-rose; and the thick perfume
  Of the locust every place.

The air and the sun and the shadows
  Were wedded and made as one;
And the winds ran over the meadows
  As little children run:

And the winds poured over the meadows
  And along the willowy way
The river ran, with its ripples shod
  With the sunshine of the day:

O the winds flowed over the meadows
  In a tide of eddies and calms,
And the bared brow felt the touch of it
  As a sweetheart's tender palms.

And the lark went palpitating
  Up through the glorious skies,
His song spilled down from the blue profound
  As a song from Paradise.

And here was the loitering current—
  Stayed by a drift of sedge
And sodden logs—scummed thick with the gold
  Of the pollen from edge to edge.

The catbird piped in the hazel,
  And the harsh kingfisher screamed;
And the crane, in amber and oozy swirls,
  Dozed in the reeds and dreamed.

And in through the tumbled driftage
  And the tangled roots below,
The waters warbled and gurgled and lisped
  Like the lips of long ago.

And the senses caught, through the music,
  Twinkles of dabbling feet,
And glimpses of faces in coverts green,
  And voices faint and sweet.

And back from the lands enchanted,
  Where my earliest mirth was born,
The trill of a laugh was blown to me
  Like the blare of an elfin horn.

Again I romped through the clover;
  And again I lay supine
On grassy swards, where the skies, like eyes,
  Looked lovingly back to mine.

And over my vision floated
  Misty illusive things—
Trailing strands of the gossamer
  On heavenward wanderings:

Figures that veered and wavered,
  Luring the sight, and then
Glancing away into nothingness,
  And blinked into shape again.

From out far depths of the forest,
  Ineffably sad and lorn,
Like the yearning cry of a long-lost love,
  The moan of the dove was borne.

And through lush glooms of the thicket
 The flash of the redbird's wings
On branches of star-white blooms that shook
 And thrilled with its twitterings.

Through mossy and viny vistas,
 Soaked ever with deepest shade,
Dimly the dull owl stared and stared
 From his bosky ambuscade.

And up through the rifted tree-tops
 That signaled the wayward breeze
I saw the hulk of the hawk becalmed
 Far out on the azure seas.

Then sudden an awe fell on me,
 As the hush of the golden day
Rounded to noon, as a May to June
 That a lover has dreamed away.

And I heard, in the breathless silence,
 And the full, glad light of the sun,
The tinkle and drip of a timorous shower—
 Ceasing as it begun.

And my thoughts, like the leaves and grasses,
 In a rapture of joy and pain,
Seemed fondled and petted and beat upon
 With a tremulous patter of rain.

Another Ride from Ghent to Aix

We sprang for the side-holts—my gripsack and I—
It dangled—I dangled—we both dangled by.
"Good speed!" cried mine host, as we landed at last—
"Speed?" chuckled the watch we went lumbering past;

Behind shut the switch, and out through the rear door
I glared while we waited a half hour more.

I had missed the express that went thundering down
Ten minutes before to my next lecture town,
And my only hope left was to catch this "wild freight,"
Which the landlord remarked was "most luckily late—
But the twenty miles distance was easily done,
If they run half as fast as they usually run!"

Not a word to each other—we struck a snail's pace—
Conductor and brakeman ne'er changing a place—
Save at the next watering-tank, where they all
Got out—strolled about—cut their names on the wall,
Or listlessly loitered on down to the pile
Of sawed wood just beyond us, to doze for a while.

'Twas high noon at starting, but while we drew near
"Arcady," I said, "We'll not make it, I fear!
I must strike Aix by eight, and it's three o'clock now;
Let me stoke up that engine, and I'll show you how!"
At which the conductor, with patience sublime,
Smiled up from his novel with, "Plenty of time!"

At "Trask," as we jolted stock-still as a stone,
I heard a cow bawl in a five o'clock tone;
And the steam from the saw-mill looked misty and thin,
And the snarl of the saw had been stifled within:
And a frowzy-haired boy, with a hat full of chips,
Came out and stared up with a smile on his lips.

At "Booneville," I groaned, "Can't I telegraph on?"
No! Why? " 'Cause the telegraph-man had just gone
To visit his folks in Almo"—and one heard
The sharp snap of my teeth through the throat of a word,
That I dragged for a mile and a half up the track,
And strangled it there, and came skulkingly back.

Again we were off. It was twilight, and more,
As we rolled o'er a bridge where beneath us the roar

Of a river came up with so wooing an air
I mechanic'ly strapped myself fast in my chair
As a brakeman slid open the door for more light,
Saying: "Captain, brace up, for your town is in sight!"

"How they'll greet me!"—and all in a moment—"che-wang!"
And the train stopped again, with a bump and a bang.
What was it? "The section-hands, just in advance."
And I spit on my hands, and I rolled up my pants,
And I clumb like an imp that the fiends had let loose
Up out of the depths of that deadly caboose.

I ran the train's length—I lept safe to the ground—
And the legend still lives that for five miles around
They heard my voice hailing the hand-car that yanked
Me aboard at my bidding, and gallantly cranked,
As I groveled and clung, with my eyes in eclipse,
And a rim of red foam round my rapturous lips.

Then I cast loose my ulster—each ear-tab let fall—
Kicked off both my shoes—let go arctics and all—
Stood up with the boys—leaned—patted each head
As it bobbed up and down with the speed that we sped;
Clapped my hands—laughed and sang—any noise, bad or good,
Till at length into Aix we rotated and stood.

And all I remember is friends flocking round
As I unsheathed my head from a hole in the ground;
And no voice but was praising that hand-car divine,
As I rubbed down its spokes with that lecture of mine,
Which (the citizens voted by common consent)
Was no more than its due. 'Twas the lecture they meant.

When the Frost Is on the Punkin

When the frost is on the punkin and the fodder's in the shock,
And you hear the kyouck and gobble of the struttin' turkey-cock
And the clackin' of the guineys, and the cluckin' of the hens,
And the rooster's hallylooyer as he tiptoes on the fence;

O, it's then's the times a feller is a-feelin' at his best,
With the risin' sun to greet him from a night of peaceful rest,
As he leaves the house, bareheaded, and goes out to feed the stock,
When the frost is on the punkin and the fodder's in the shock.

They's something kindo' harty-like about the atmusfere
When the heat of summer's over and the coolin' fall is here—
Of course we miss the flowers, and the blossums on the trees,
And the mumble of the hummin'-birds and buzzin' of the bees;
But the air's so appetizin'; and the landscape through the haze
Of a crisp and sunny morning of the airly autumn days
Is a pictur' that no painter has the colorin' to mock—
When the frost is on the punkin and the fodder's in the shock.

The husky, rusty russel of the tossels of the corn,
And the raspin' of the tangled leaves, as golden as the morn;
The stubble in the furries—kindo' lonesome-like, but still
A-preachin' sermons to us of the barns they growed to fill;
The strawstack in the medder, and the reaper in the shed;
The hosses in theyr stalls below—the clover overhead!—
O, it sets my hart a-clickin' like the tickin' of a clock,
When the frost is on the punkin and the fodder's in the shock!

Then your apples all is gethered, and the ones a feller keeps
Is poured around the celler-floor in red and yeller heaps;
And your cider-makin' 's over, and your wimmern-folks is through
With their mince and apple-butter, and theyr souse and saussage,
too!
I don't know how to tell it—but ef sich a thing could be
As the Angels wantin' boardin', and they'd call around on *me*—
I'd want to 'commodate 'em—all the whole-indurin' flock—
When the frost is on the punkin and the fodder's in the shock!

A Dream of Autumn

Mellow hazes, lowly trailing
Over wood and meadow, veiling
Somber skies, with wild fowl sailing
Sailor-like to foreign lands;

And the north wind overleaping
Summer's brink, and flood-like sweeping
Wrecks of roses where the weeping-
  Willows wring their helpless hands.

Flared, like Titan torches flinging
Flakes of flame and embers, springing
From the vale, the trees stand swinging
  In the moaning atmosphere;
While in dead'ning lands the lowing
Of the cattle, sadder growing,
Fills the sense to overflowing
  With the sorrow of the year.

Sorrowfully, yet the sweeter
Sings the brook in rippled meter
Under boughs that lithely teeter
  Lorn birds, answering from the shores
Through the viny, shady-shiny
Interspaces, shot with tiny
Flying motes that fleck the winy
  Wave-engraven sycamores.

Fields of ragged stubble, wrangled
With rank weeds, and shocks of tangled
Corn, with crests like rent plumes dangled
  Over Harvest's battle-plain;
And the sudden whir and whistle
Of the quail that, like a missile,
Whizzes over thorn and thistle,
  And, a missile, drops again.

Muffled voices, hid in thickets
Where the redbird stops to stick its
Ruddy beak betwixt the pickets
  Of the truant's rustic trap;
And the sound of laughter ringing
Where, within the wild vine swinging,
Climb Bacchante's schoolmates, flinging
  Purple clusters in her lap.

Rich as wine, the sunset flashes
Round the tilted world, and dashes
Up the sloping West, and splashes
  Red foam over sky and sea—
Till my dream of Autumn, paling
In the splendor all-prevailing,
Like a sallow leaf goes sailing
  Down the silence solemnly.

from A Child-World

PROEM

The Child-World—long and long since lost to view—
A Fairy Paradise!—
How always fair it was and fresh and new—
How every affluent hour heaped heart and eyes
With treasures of surprise!

Enchantments tangible: The under-brink
Of dawns that launched the sight
Up seas of gold: The dewdrop on the pink,
With all the green earth in it and blue height
Of heavens infinite:

The liquid, dripping songs of orchard-birds—
The wee bass of the bees,—
With lucent deeps of silence afterwards;
The gay, clandestine whisperings of the breeze
And glad leaves of the trees.

. . . .

O Child-World: After this world—just as when
I found you first sufficed
My soulmost need—if I found you again,
With all my childish dream so realized,
I should not be surprised.

THE CHILD-WORLD

A Child-World, yet a wondrous world no less,
To those who knew its boundless happiness.
A simple old frame house — eight rooms in all —
Set just one side the center of a small
But very hopeful Indiana town, —
The upper story looking squarely down
Upon the main street, and the main highway
From East to West, — historic in its day,
Known as The National Road — old-timers, all
Who linger yet, will happily recall
It as the scheme and handiwork, as well
As property, of "Uncle Sam," and tell
Of its importance, "long and long afore
*Rail*roads wuz ever *dreamp'* of!" — Furthermore,
The reminiscent first inhabitants
Will make that old road blossom with romance
Of snowy caravans, in long parade
Of covered vehicles, of every grade
From ox-cart of most primitive design,
To Conestoga wagons, with their fine
Deep-chested six-horse teams, in heavy gear,
High hames and chiming bells — to childish ear
And eye entrancing as the glittering train
Of some sun-smitten pageant of old Spain.
And, in like spirit, haply they will tell
You of the roadside forests, and the yell
Of "wolfs" and "painters," in the long night-ride,
And "screechin' catamounts" on every side. —
Of stage-coach days, highwaymen, and strange crimes,
And yet unriddled mysteries of the times
Called "Good Old." "And why 'Good Old'?" once a rare
Old chronicler was asked, who brushed the hair
Out of his twinkling eyes and said, — "Well, John,
They're 'good old times' because they're dead and gone!"

The old home site was portioned into three
Distinctive lots. The front one — natively

Facing to southward, broad and gaudy-fine
With lilac, dahlia, rose, and flowering vine—
The dwelling stood in; and behind that, and
Upon the alley north and south, left hand,
The old woodhouse,—half, trimly stacked with wood,
And half, a workshop, where a workbench stood
Steadfastly through all seasons.—Over it,
Along the wall, hung compass, brace-and-bit,
And square, and drawing-knife, and smoothing-plane—
And a little jack-plane, too—the children's vain
Possession by pretense—in fancy they
Manipulating it in endless play,
Turning out countless curls and loops of bright,
Fine satin shavings—Rapture infinite!
Shelved quilting-frames; the tool-chest; the old box
Of refuse nails and screws; a rough gun-stock's
Outline in "curly maple"; and a pair
Of clamps and old kraut-cutter hanging there.
Some "patterns," in thin wood, of shield and scroll,
Hung higher, with a neat "cane fishing-pole"
And careful tackle—all securely out
Of reach of children, rummaging about.

Beside the woodhouse, with broad branches free
Yet close above the roof, an apple tree
Known as "The Prince's Harvest"—Magic phrase!
That was *a boy's own tree*, in many ways!—
Its girth and height meet both for the caress
Of his bare legs and his ambitiousness:
And then its apples, humoring his whim,
Seemed just to fairly *hurry* ripe for him—
Even in June, impetuous as he,
They dropped to meet him, half-way up the tree.
And O their bruised sweet faces where they fell!—
And ho! the lips that feigned to "kiss them *well*"!

"The Old Sweet-Apple Tree," a stalwart, stood
In fairly sympathetic neighborhood
Of this wild princeling with his early gold
To toss about so lavishly nor hold

In bounteous hoard to overbrim at once
All Nature's lap when came the Autumn months.
Under the spacious shade of this the eyes
Of swinging children saw swift-changing skies
Of blue and green, with sunshine shot between,
And when "the old cat died" they saw but green.

And, then, there was a cherry tree.—We all
And severally will yet recall
From our lost youth, in gentlest memory,
The blessed fact—There was a cherry tree.

There was a cherry tree. Its bloomy snows
Cool even now the fevered sight that knows
No more its airy visions of pure joy—
As when you were a boy.

There was a cherry tree. The Bluejay set
His blue against its white—O blue as jet
He seemed there then!—But *now*—Whoever knew
He was so pale a blue!

There was a cherry tree—Our child-eyes saw
The miracle:—Its pure-white snows did thaw
Into a crimson fruitage, far too sweet
But for a boy to eat.

There was a cherry tree, give thanks and joy!—
There was a bloom of snow—There was a boy—
There was a Bluejay of the realest blue—
And fruit for both of you.

Then the old garden, with the apple trees
Grouped round the margin, and "a stand of bees"
By the "white-winter-pearmain"; and a row
Of currant-bushes; and a quince or so.
The old grape-arbor in the center, by
The pathway to the stable, with the sty
Behind it, and *upon* it, cootering flocks
Of pigeons,—and the cutest "martin-box"!—
Made like a sure-enough house—with roof, and doors
And windows in it, and veranda-floors

And balusters all round it—yes, and at
Each end a chimney—painted red at that
And penciled white, to look like little bricks;
And, to cap all the builder's cunning tricks,
Two tiny little lightning-rods were run
Straight up their sides, and twinkled in the sun.
Who built it? Nay, no answer but a smile.—
It *may* be you can guess who, after while.

Home in his stall, "Old Sorrel" munched his hay
And oats and corn, and switched the flies away,
In a repose of patience good to see,
And earnest of the gentlest pedigree.
With half-pathetic eye sometimes he gazed
Upon the gambols of a colt that grazed
Around the edges of the lot outside,
And kicked at nothing suddenly, and tried
To act grown-up and graceful and high-bred,
But dropped, *k'whop!* and scraped the buggy-shed,
Leaving a tuft of woolly, foxy hair
Under the sharp end of a gate-hinge there.
Then, all ignobly scrambling to his feet
And whinnying a whinny like a bleat,
He would pursue himself around the lot
And—do the whole thing over, like as not! . . .
Ah! what a life of constant fear and dread
And flop and squawk and flight the chickens led!

Above the fences, either side, were seen
The neighbor-houses, set in plots of green
Dooryards and greener gardens, tree and wall
Alike whitewashed, an order in it all:
The scythe hooked in the tree-fork; and the spade
And hoe and rake and shovel all, when laid
Aside, were in their places, ready for
The hand of either the possessor or
Of any neighbor, welcome to the loan
Of any tool he might not chance to own.

THE OLD HOME-FOLKS

Such was the Child-World of the long ago—
The little world these children used to know:—
Johnty, the oldest, and the best, perhaps,
Of the five happy little Hoosier chaps
Inhabiting this wee world all their own.—
Johnty, the leader, with his native tone
Of grave command—a general on parade
Whose each punctilious order was obeyed
By his proud followers.

But Johnty yet—
After all serious duties—could forget
The gravity of life to the extent,
At times, of kindling much astonishment
About him: With a quick, observant eye,
And mind and memory, he could supply
The tamest incident with liveliest mirth;
And at the most unlooked-for times on earth
Was wont to break into some travesty
On those around him—feats of mimicry
Of this one's trick of gesture—that one's walk—
Or this one's laugh—or that one's funny talk,—
The way "the watermelon-man" would try
His humor on town-folks that wouldn't buy;—
How he drove into town at morning—then
At dusk (alas!) how he drove out again.
Though these divertisements of Johnty's were
Hailed with a hearty glee and relish, there
Appeared a sense, on his part, of regret—
A spirit of remorse that would not let
Him rest for days thereafter.—Such times he,
As some boy said, "jist got too overly
Blame' good fer common boys like us, you know
To *'so*ciate with—'less'n we 'ud go
And jine his church!"

Next after Johnty came
His little towhead brother, Bud by name.—
And O how white his hair was—and how thick
His face with freckles,—and his ears, how quick
And curious and intrusive!—And how pale
The blue of his big eyes;—and how a tale
Of Giants, Trolls or Fairies, bulged them still
Bigger and bigger!—And when "Jack" would kill
The old "Four-headed Giant," Bud's big eyes
Were swollen truly into giant-size.
And Bud was apt in make-believes—would hear
His Grandma talk or read, with such an ear
And memory of both subject and big words,
That he would take the book up afterwards
And feign to "read aloud," with such success
As caused his truthful elders real distress.
But he *must* have *big words*—they seemed to give
Extremer range to the superlative—
That was his passion. "My Gran'ma," he said,
One evening, after listening as she read
Some heavy old historical review—
With copious explanations thereunto
Drawn out by his inquiring turn of mind,—
"My Gran'ma she's read *all* books—ever' kind
They is, 'at tells all 'bout the land an' sea
An' Nations of the Earth!—An' she is the
Historicul-est woman ever wuz!"
(Forgive the verse's chuckling as it does
In its erratic current.—Oftentimes
The little willowy water-brook of rhymes
Must falter in its music, listening to
The children laughing as they used to do.)

Who shall sing a simple ditty all about the Willow,
Dainty-fine and delicate as any bending spray
That dandles high the happy bird that flutters there to trill a
Tremulously tender song of greeting to the May.

Bravest, too, of all the trees!—none to match your daring,—
First of greens to greet the Spring and lead in leafy sheen;—
Ay, and you're the last—almost into winter wearing
Still the leaf of loyalty—still the badge of green.

Ah, my lovely Willow! — Let the Waters lilt your graces, —
They alone with limpid kisses lave your leaves above,
Flashing back your sylvan beauty, and in shady places
Peering up with glimmering pebbles, like the eyes of love.

Next, Maymie, with her hazy cloud of hair,
And the blue skies of eyes beneath it there.
Her dignified and "little lady" airs
Of never either romping up the stairs
Or falling down them; thoughtful every way
Of others first — The kind of child at play
That "gave up," for the rest, the ripest pear
Or peach or apple in the garden there
Beneath the trees where swooped the airy swing —
She pushing it, too glad for anything!
Or, in the character of hostess, she
Would entertain her friends delightfully
In her playhouse, — with strips of carpet laid
Along the garden-fence within the shade
Of the old apple trees — where from next yard
Came the two dearest friends in her regard,
The little Crawford girls, Ella and Lu —
As shy and lovely as the lilies grew
In their idyllic home, — yet sometimes they
Admitted Bud and Alex to their play,
Who did their heavier work and helped them fix
To have a "Festibul" — and brought the bricks
And built the "stove," with a real fire and all,
And stovepipe-joint for chimney, looming tall
And wonderfully smoky — even to
Their childish aspirations, as it blew
And swooped and swirled about them till their sight
Was feverish even as their high delight.

Then Alex, with his freckles, and his freaks
Of temper, and the peach-bloom of his cheeks,
And "*amber-colored* hair" — his mother said
'Twas that, when others laughed and called it "*red*"
And Alex threw things at them — till they'd call

A truce, agreeing " 't'uzn't red *ut-tall!*"
But Alex was affectionate beyond
The average child, and was extremely fond
Of the paternal relatives of his,
Of whom he once made estimate like this: —
"*I'm* only got *two* brothers, — but my *Pa*
He's got most brothers'n you ever saw! —
He's got *seben* brothers! — Yes, an' they're all my
Seben Uncles! — Uncle John, an' Jim, — an' I
Got Uncle George, an' Uncle Andy, too,
An' Uncle Frank, an' Uncle Joe. — An' you
Know Uncle *Mart.* — An', all but *him*, they're great
Big mens! — An' nen's Aunt Sarah — she makes eight! —
I'm got *eight* uncles! — 'cept Aunt Sarah *can't*
Be ist my *uncle* 'cause she's ist my *a'nt!*"

Then, next to Alex — and the last indeed
Of these five little ones of whom you read —
Was baby Lizzie, with her velvet lisp, —
As though her elfin lips had caught some wisp
Of floss between them as they strove with speech,
Which ever seemed just in, yet out of, reach —
Though what her lips missed, her dark eyes could say
With looks that made her meaning clear as day.
And, knowing now the children, you must know
The father and the mother they loved so: —
The father was a swarthy man, black-eyed,
Black-haired, and high of forehead; and, beside
The slender little mother, seemed in truth
A very king of men — since, from his youth,
To his hale manhood *now* — (worthy as then, —
A lawyer and a leading citizen
Of the proud little town and county-seat —
His hopes his neighbors', and their fealty sweet) —
He had known outdoor labor — rain and shine —
Bleak Winter, and bland Summer — foul and fine.
So Nature had ennobled him and set
Her symbol on him like a coronet:
His lifted brow, and frank, reliant face —
Superior of stature as of grace, —

Even the children by the spell were wrought
Up to heroics of their simple thought,
And saw him, trim of build, and lithe and straight
And tall, almost, as at the pasture-gate
The towering ironweed the scythe had spared
For their sakes, when The Hired Man declared
It would grow on till it became a *tree*,
With cocoanuts and monkeys in — maybe!

Yet, though the children, in their pride and awe
And admiration of the father, saw
A being so exalted — even more
Like adoration was the love they bore
The gentle mother. — Her mild, plaintive face
Was purely fair, and haloed with a grace
And sweetness luminous when joy made glad
Her features with a smile; or saintly sad
As twilight, fell the sympathetic gloom
Of any childish grief, or as a room
Were darkened suddenly, the curtain drawn
Across the window and the sunshine gone.
Her brow, below her fair hair's glimmering strands,
Seemed meetest resting-place for blessing hands
Or holiest touches of soft finger-tips
And little rose-leaf cheeks and dewy lips.

Though heavy household tasks were pitiless,
No little waist or coat or checkered dress
But knew her needle's deftness; and no skill
Matched hers in shaping plait or flounce or frill;
Or fashioning, in complicate design,
All rich embroideries of leaf and vine,
With tiniest twining tendril, — bud and bloom
And fruit, so like, one's fancy caught perfume
And dainty touch and taste of them, to see
Their semblance wrought in such rare verity.

Shrined in her sanctity of home and love,
And love's fond service and reward thereof,
Restore her thus, O blessed Memory! —

Throned in her rocking-chair, and on her knee
Her sewing — her work-basket on the floor
Beside her, — Spring-time through the open door
Balmily stealing in and all about
The room; the bees' dim hum, and the far shout
And laughter of the children at their play
And neighbor children from across the way
Calling in gleeful challenge — save alone
One boy whose voice sends back no answering tone —
The boy, prone on the floor, above a book
Of pictures, with a rapt, ecstatic look —
Even as the mother's, by the selfsame spell,
Is lifted, with a light ineffable —
As though her senses caught no mortal cry,
But heard, instead, some poem going by.

The Child-heart is so strange a little thing —
So mild — so timorously shy and small, —
When *grown-up* hearts throb, it goes scampering
Behind the wall, nor dares peer out at all! —
It is the veriest mouse
That hides in any house —
So wild a little thing is any Child-heart!

Child-heart! — mild heart! —
Ho, my little wild heart! —
Come up here to me out o' the dark,
Or let me come to you!

So lorn at times the Child-heart needs must be
With never one maturer heart for friend
And comrade, whose tear-ripened sympathy
And love might lend it comfort to the end, —
Whose yearnings, aches and stings,
Over poor little things
Were pitiful as ever any Child-heart.

Child-heart! — mild heart! —
Ho, my little wild heart! —
Come up here to me out o' the dark,
Or let me come to you!

Times, too, the little Child-heart must be glad —
Being so young, nor knowing, as *we* know,
The fact from fantasy, the good from bad,

The joy from woe, the—*all* that hurts us so!
What wonder then that thus
It hides away from us?—
So weak a little thing is any Child-heart!

Child-heart!—mild heart!—
Ho, my little wild heart!—
Come up here to me out o' the dark,
Or let me come to you!

Nay, little Child-heart, you have never need
To fear *us;*—we are weaker far than you—
'Tis *we* who should be fearful—we indeed
Should hide us, too, as darkly as you do,—
Safe, as yourself, withdrawn,
Hearing the World roar on
Too wilful, woeful, awful for the Child-heart!

Child-heart!—mild heart!—
Ho, my little wild heart!—
Come up here to me out o' the dark,
Or let me come to you!

The clock chats on confidingly; a rose
Taps at the window, as the sunlight throws
A brilliant, jostling checkerwork of shine
And shadow, like a Persian-loom design,
Across the home-made carpet—fades,—and then
The dear old colors are themselves again.
Sounds drop in visiting from everywhere—
The bluebird's and the robin's trill are there,
Their sweet liquidity diluted some
By dewy orchard-spaces they have come:
Sounds of the town, too, and the great highway—
The Mover-wagons' rumble, and the neigh
Of over-traveled horses, and the bleat
Of sheep and low of cattle through the street—
A Nation's thoroughfare of hopes and fears,
First blazed by the heroic pioneers
Who gave up old-home idols and set face
Toward the unbroken West, to found a race
And tame a wilderness now mightier than
All peoples and all tracts American.

Blent with all outer sounds, the sounds within:—
In mild remoteness falls the household din
Of porch and kitchen: the dull jar and thump
Of churning; and the "glung-glung" of the pump,
With sudden pad and skurry of bare feet
Of little outlaws, in from field or street:
The clang of kettle,—rasp of damper-ring
And bang of cook-stove door—and everything
That jingles in a busy kitchen lifts
Its individual wrangling voice and drifts
In sweetest tinny, coppery, pewtery tone
Of music hungry ear has ever known
In wildest famished yearning and conceit
Of youth, to just cut loose and eat and eat!—
The zest of hunger still incited on
To childish desperation by long-drawn
Breaths of hot, steaming, wholesome things that stew
And blubber, and uptilt the pot-lids, too,
Filling the sense with zestful rumors of
The dear old-fashioned dinners children love:
Redolent savorings of home-cured meats,
Potatoes, beans and cabbage; turnips, beets
And parsnips—rarest composite entire
That ever pushed a mortal child's desire
To madness by new-grated fresh, keen, sharp
Horseradish—tang that sets the lips awarp
And watery, anticipating all
The cloyed sweets of the glorious festival.—
Still add the cinnamony, spicy scents
Of clove, nutmeg, and myriad condiments
In like-alluring whiffs that prophesy
Of sweltering pudding, cake, and custard-pie—
The swooning-sweet aroma haunting all
The house—up-stairs and down—porch, parlor, hall
And sitting-room—invading even where
The Hired Man sniffs it in the orchard-air,
And pauses in his pruning of the trees
To note the sun minutely and to—sneeze.

Then Cousin Rufus comes—the children hear

His hale voice in the old hall, ringing clear
As any bell. Always he came with song
Upon his lips and all the happy throng
Of echoes following him, even as the crowd
Of his admiring little kinsmen—proud
To have a cousin *grown*—and yet as young
Of soul and cheery as the songs he sung.

He was a student of the law—intent
Soundly to win success, with all it meant;
And so he studied—even as he played,—
With all his heart: And so it was he made
His gallant fight for fortune—through all stress
Of battle bearing him with cheeriness
And wholesome valor.

And the children had
Another relative who kept them glad
And joyous by his very merry ways—
As blithe and sunny as the summer days,—
Their father's youngest brother—Uncle Mart.
The old "Arabian Nights" he knew by heart—
"Baron Munchausen," too; and likewise "The
Swiss Family Robinson."—And when these three
Gave out, as he rehearsed them, he could go
Straight on in the same line—a steady flow
Of arabesque invention that his good
Old mother never clearly understood.
He *was* to be a *printer*—wanted, though,
To be an *actor*.—But the world was "show"
Enough for *him*,—theatric, airy, gay,—
Each day to him was jolly as a play.
And some poetic symptoms, too, in sooth,
Were certain.—And, from his apprentice youth,
He joyed in verse-quotations—which he took
Out of the old "Type Foundry Specimen Book."
He craved and courted most the favor of
The children.—They were foremost in his love;
And pleasing *them*, he pleased his own boy-heart
And kept it young and fresh in every part.

So was it he devised for them and wrought
To life his quaintest, most romantic thought:—
Like some lone castaway in alien seas,
He built a house up in the apple trees,
Out in the corner of the garden, where
No man-devouring native, prowling there,
Might pounce upon them in the dead o' night—
For lo, their little ladder, slim and light,
They drew up after them. And it was known
That Uncle Mart slipped up sometimes alone
And drew the ladder in, to lie and moon
Over some novel all the afternoon.
And one time Johnty, from the crowd below,—
Outraged to find themselves deserted so—
Threw bodily their old black cat up in
The airy fastness, with much yowl and din
Resulting, while a wild periphery
Of cat went circling to another tree,
And, in impassioned outburst, Uncle Mart
Loomed up, and thus relieved his tragic heart:

" '*Hence, long-tailed, ebon-eyed, nocturnal ranger!*
What led thee hither 'mongst the types and cases?
Didst thou not know that running midnight races
O'er standing types was fraught with imminent danger?
Did hunger lead thee—didst thou think to find
Some rich old cheese to fill thy hungry maw?
Vain hope! for none but literary jaw
Can masticate our cookery for the mind!' "

So likewise when, with lordly air and grace,
He strode to dinner, with a tragic face
With ink-spots on it from the office, he
Would aptly quote more "Specimen-poetry"—
Perchance like " 'Labor's bread is sweet to eat,
(*Ahem!*) And toothsome is the toiler's meat.' "

Ah, could you see them *all*, at lull of noon!—
A sort of *boisterous* lull, with clink of spoon
And clatter of deflecting knife, and plate

Dropped saggingly, with its all-bounteous weight,
And dragged in place voraciously; and then
Pent exclamations, and the lull again.—
The garland of glad faces round the board—
Each member of the family restored
To his or her place, with an extra chair
Or two for the chance guests so often there.—
The father's farmer-client, brought home from
The court room, though he "didn't *want* to come
Tel he jist saw he *hat* to!" he'd explain,
Invariably, time and time again,
To the pleased wife and hostess, as she pressed
Another cup of coffee on the guest.—
Or there was Johnty's special chum, perchance,
Or Bud's, or both—each childish countenance
Lit with a higher glow of youthful glee,
To be together thus unbrokenly,—
Jim Offutt, or Eck Skinner, or George Carr—
The very nearest chums of Bud's these are,—
So, very probably, *one* of the three,
At least, is there with Bud, or *ought* to be.
Like interchange the town-boys each had known—
His playmate's dinner better than his own—
Yet blest that he was ever made to stay
At *Almon Keefer's any* blessed day,
For *any* meal! . . . Visions of biscuits, hot
And flaky-perfect, with the golden blot
Of molten butter for the center, clear,
Through pools of clover-honey—*dear-o-dear!*—
With creamy milk for its divine "farewell":
And then, if any one delectable
Might yet exceed in sweetness, O restore
The cherry-cobbler of the days of yore
Made only by Al Keefer's mother!—Why,
The very thought of it ignites the eye
Of memory with rapture—cloys the lip
Of longing, till it seems to ooze and drip
With veriest juice and stain and overwaste
Of that most sweet delirium of taste
That ever visited the childish tongue,

Or proved, as now, the sweetest thing unsung.
Ah, Almon Keefer! what a boy you were,
With your back-tilted hat and careless hair,
And open, honest, fresh, fair face and eyes
With their all-varying looks of pleased surprise
And joyous interest in flower and tree,
And poising humming-bird, and maundering bee.
The fields and woods he knew; the tireless tramp
With gun and dog; and the night-fisher's camp—
No other boy, save Bee Lineback, had won
Such brilliant mastery of rod and gun.
Even in his earliest childhood had he shown
These traits that marked him as his father's own.
Dogs all paid Almon honor and bow-wowed
Allegiance, let him come in any crowd
Of rabbit-hunting town-boys, even though
His own dog "Sleuth" rebuked their acting so
With jealous snarls and growlings.

But the best
Of Almon's virtues—leading all the rest—
Was his great love of books, and skill as well
In reading them aloud, and by the spell
Thereof enthralling his mute listeners, as
They grouped about him in the orchard-grass,
Hinging their bare shins in the mottled shine
And shade, as they lay prone, or stretched supine
Beneath their favorite tree, with dreamy eyes
And Argo-fancies voyaging the skies.
"Tales of the Ocean" was the name of one
Old dog's-eared book that was surpassed by none
Of all the glorious list.—Its back was gone,
But its vitality went bravely on
In such delicious tales of land and sea
As may not ever perish utterly.
Of still more dubious caste, "Jack Sheppard" drew
Full admiration; and "Dick Turpin," too.
And, painful as the fact is to convey,
In certain lurid tales of their own day,
These boys found thieving heroes and outlaws

They hailed with equal fervor of applause:
"The League of the Miami"—why, the name
Alone was fascinating—is the same,
In memory, this venerable hour
Of moral wisdom shorn of all its power,
As it unblushingly reverts to when
The old barn was "the Cave," and hears again
The signal blown, outside the buggy-shed—
The drowsy guard within uplifts his head,
And " '*Who goes there?*' " is called, in bated breath—
The challenge answered in a hush of death,—
"Sh!—'*Barney Gray!*' " And then " '*What do you seek?*' "
" '*Stables of The League!*' " the voice comes spent and weak,
For, ha! the *Law* is on the "Chieftain's" trail—
Tracked to his very lair!—Well, what avail?
The "secret entrance" opens—closes.—So
The "Robber-Captain" thus outwits his foe;
And, safe once more within his "cavern-halls,"
He shakes his clenched fist at the warped plank-walls
And mutters his defiance through the cracks
At the balked Enemy's retreating backs
As the loud horde flees pell-mell down the lane,
And—*Almon Keefer* is himself again!

Excepting few, they were not books indeed
Of deep import that Almon chose to read;—
Less fact than fiction.—Much he favored those—
If not in poetry, in hectic prose—
That made our native Indian a wild,
Feathered and fine-preened hero that a child
Could recommend as just about the thing
To make a god of, or at least a king.

Aside from Almon's own books—two or three—
His store of lore The Township Library
Supplied him weekly: All the books with "or's"
Subtitled—lured him—after "Indian Wars,"
And "Life of Daniel Boone,"—not to include
Some few books spiced with humor,—"Robin Hood"
And rare "Don Quixote."—And one time he took

"Dadd's Cattle Doctor." . . . How he hugged the book
And hurried homeward, with internal glee
And humorous spasms of expectancy! —
All this confession — as he promptly made
It, the day later, writhing in the shade
Of the old apple tree with Johnty and
Bud, Noey Bixler, and The Hired Hand —
Was quite as funny as the book was not. . . .
O Wonderland of wayward Childhood! what
An easy, breezy realm of summer calm
And dreamy gleam and gloom and bloom and balm
Thou art! — The Lotus-Land the poet sung,
It is the Child-World while the heart beats young. . . .

While the heart beats young! — O the splendor of the Spring,
With all her dewy jewels on, is not so fair a thing!
The fairest, rarest morning of the blossom-time of May
Is not so sweet a season as the season of to-day
While Youth's diviner climate folds and holds us, close caressed
As we feel our mothers with us by the touch of face and breast; —
Our bare feet in the meadows, and our fancies up among
The airy clouds of morning — while the heart beats young.

While the heart beats young and our pulses leap and dance,
With every day a holiday and life a glad romance, —
We hear the birds with wonder, and with wonder watch their flight —
Standing still the more enchanted, both of hearing and of sight,
When they have vanished wholly, — for, in fancy, wing-to-wing
We fly to Heaven with them; and, returning, still we sing
The praises of this *lower* Heaven with tireless voice and tongue,
Even as the Master sanctions — while the heart beats young.

While the heart beats young! — While the heart beats young!
O green and gold old Earth of ours, with azure overhung
And looped with rainbows! — grant us yet this grassy lap of thine —
We would be still thy children, through the shower and the shine!
So pray we, lisping, whispering, in childish love and trust,
With our beseeching hands and faces lifted from the dust
By fervor of the poem, all unwritten and unsung,
Thou givest us in answer, while the heart beats young.

Another hero of those youthful years
Returns, as Noey Bixler's name appears.
And Noey — if in any special way —

Was notably good-natured.—Work or play
He entered into with selfsame delight—
A wholesome interest that made him quite
As many friends among the old as young,—
So everywhere were Noey's praises sung.

And he was awkward, fat and overgrown,
With a round full-moon face, that fairly shone
As though to meet the simile's demand.
And, cumbrous though he seemed, both eye and hand
Were dowered with the discernment and deft skill
Of the true artisan: He shaped at will,
In his old father's shop, on rainy days,
Little toy-wagons, and curved-runner sleighs;
The trimmest bows and arrows—fashioned, too,
Of "seasoned timber," such as Noey knew
How to select, prepare, and then complete,
And call his little friends in from the street.
"The very *best* bow," Noey used to say,
"Hain't made o' ash ner hick'ry thataway!—
But you git *mulberry*—the *bearin'*-tree,
Now mind ye! and you fetch the piece to me,
And lemme git it *seasoned*; then, i gum!
I'll make a bow 'at you kin brag on some!
Er—ef you can't git *mulberry*,—you bring
Me a' old *locus'* hitch-post, and, i jing!
I'll make a bow o' *that* 'at *common* bows
Won't dast to pick on ner turn up their nose!"

And Noey knew the woods, and all the trees
And thickets, plants and myriad mysteries
Of swamp and bottom-land. And he knew where
The ground-hog hid, and why located there.—
He knew all animals that burrowed, swam,
Or lived in tree-tops: And, by race and dam,
He knew the choicest, safest deeps wherein
Fish-traps might flourish nor provoke the sin
Of theft in some chance peeking, prying sneak,
Or town-boy, prowling up and down the creek.
All four-pawed creatures tamable—he knew

Their outer and their inner natures too;
While they, in turn, were drawn to him as by
Some subtle recognition of a tie
Of love, as true as truth from end to end,
Between themselves and this strange human friend.
The same with birds — he knew them every one
And he could "name them, too, without a gun."
No wonder *Johnty* loved him, even to
The verge of worship. — Noey led him through
The art of trapping redbirds — yes, and taught
Him how to keep them when he had them caught —
What food they needed, and just where to swing
The cage, if he expected them to *sing*.

And *Bud* loved Noey, for the little pair
Of stilts he made him; or the stout old hair
Trunk Noey put on wheels, and laid a track
Of scantling-railroad for it in the back
Part of the barn-lot; or the crossbow, made
Just like a gun, which deadly weapon laid
Against his shoulder as he aimed, and — "*Sping!*"
He'd hear the rusty old nail zoon and sing —
And *zip!* your Mr. Bluejay's wing would drop
A farewell-feather from the old tree-top!

And *Maymie* loved him, for the very small
But perfect carriage for her favorite doll —
A *lady's* carriage — not a *baby*-cab, —
But oil-cloth top, and two seats, lined with drab
And trimmed with white lace-paper from a case
Of shaving-soap his uncle bought some place
At auction once.

And *Alex* loved him yet
The best, when Noey brought him, for a pet,
A little flying-squirrel, with great eyes —
Big as a child's: And, childlike otherwise,
It was at first a timid, tremulous, coy,
Retiring little thing that dodged the boy
And tried to keep in Noey's pocket; — till,

In time responsive to his patient will,
It became wholly docile, and content
With its new master, as he came and went,—
The squirrel clinging flatly to his breast,
Or sometimes scampering its craziest
Around his body spirally, and then
Down to his very heels and up again.

And *Little Lizzie* loved him, as a bee
Loves a great ripe red apple—utterly.
For Noey's ruddy morning-face she drew
The window-blind, and tapped the window, too;
Afar she hailed his coming, as she heard
His tuneless whistling—sweet as any bird
It seemed to her, the one lame bar or so
Of old "Wait for the Wagon"—hoarse and low
The sound was,—so that, all about the place,
Folks joked and said that Noey "whistled bass"—
The light remark originally made
By Cousin Rufus, who knew notes, and played
The flute with nimble skill, and taste as well,
And, critical as he was musical,
Regarded Noey's constant whistling thus
"Phenomenally unmelodious."
Likewise when Uncle Mart, who shared the love
Of jest with Cousin Rufus hand-in-glove,
Said "Noey couldn't whistle *'Bonny Doon'*
Even! and, *he'd* bet, couldn't carry a tune
If it had handles to it!"

—But forgive
The deviations here so fugitive,
And turn again to Little Lizzie, whose
High estimate of Noey we shall choose
Above all others.—And to her he was
Particularly lovable because
He laid the woodland's harvest at her feet.—
He brought her wild strawberries, honey-sweet
And dewy-cool, in mats of greenest moss
And leaves, all woven over and across

With tender, biting "tongue-grass," and "sheep-sour,"
And twin-leaved beech-mast, pranked with bud and flower
Of every gipsy-blossom of the wild,
Dark, tangled forest, dear to any child.—
All these in season. Nor could barren, drear,
White and stark-featured Winter interfere
With Noey's rare resources: Still the same
He blithely whistled through the snow and came
Beneath the window with a Fairy sled;
And Little Lizzie, bundled heels-and-head,
He took on such excursions of delight
As even "Old Santy" with his reindeer might
Have envied her! And, later, when the snow
Was softening toward Spring-time and the glow
Of steady sunshine smote upon it,—then
Came the magician Noey yet again—
While all the children were away a day
Or two at Grandma's!—and behold when they
Got home once more;—there, towering taller than
The doorway—stood a mighty, old Snow-Man!
A thing of peerless art—a masterpiece
Doubtless unmatched by even classic Greece
In heyday of Praxiteles.—Alone
It loomed in lordly grandeur all its own.
And steadfast, too, for weeks and weeks it stood,
The admiration of the neighborhood
As well as of the children Noey sought
Only to honor in the work he wrought.
The traveler paid it tribute, as he passed
Along the highway—paused and, turning, cast
A lingering, last look—as though to take
A vivid print of it, for memory's sake,
To lighten all the empty, aching miles
Beyond with brighter fancies, hopes and smiles.
The cynic put aside his biting wit
And tacitly declared in praise of it;
And even the apprentice-poet of the town
Rose to impassioned heights, and then sat down
And penned a panegyric scroll of rhyme
That made the Snow-Man famous for all time.

And though, as now, the ever warmer sun
Of summer had so melted and undone
The perishable figure that—alas!—
Not even in dwindled white against the grass
Was left its latest and minutest ghost,
The children yet—*materially*, almost—
Beheld it—circled round it hand-in-hand—
(Or rather round the place it used to stand)—
With "Ring-a-round-a-rosy! Bottle full
O' posy!" and, with shriek and laugh, would pull
From seeming contact with it—just as when
It was the *real-est* of old Snow-Men!

Even in such a scene of senseless play
The children were surprised one summer day
By a strange man who called across the fence,
Inquiring for their father's residence;
And, being answered that this was the place,
Opened the gate, and, with a radiant face,
Came in and sat down with them in the shade
And waited—till the absent father made
His noon appearance, with a warmth and zest
That told he had no ordinary guest
In this man whose low-spoken name he knew
At once, demurring as the stranger drew
A stuffy note-book out, and turned and set
A big fat finger on a page, and let
The writing thereon testify instead
Of further speech. And as the father read
All silently, the curious children took
Exacting inventory both of book
And man:—He wore a long-napped white fur hat
Pulled firmly on his head, and under that
Rather long silvery hair, or iron-gray—
For he was not an old man,—anyway,
Not beyond sixty. And he wore a pair
Of square-framed spectacles—or rather there
Were two more than a pair,—the extra two
Flared at the corners, at the eyes' side-view,
In as redundant vision as the eyes

Of grasshoppers or bees or dragon-flies.
Later the children heard the father say
He was "A Noted Traveler," and would stay
Some days with them. — In which time host and guest
Discussed, alone, in deepest interest,
Some vague, mysterious matter that defied
The wistful children, loitering outside
The spare-room door. There Bud acquired a quite
New list of big words — such as "Disunite,"
And "Shibboleth," and "Aristocracy,"
And "Juggernaut," and "Squatter Sovereignty,"
And "Antislavery," "Emancipate,"
"Irrepressible Conflict," and "The Great
Battle of Armageddon" — obviously
A pamphlet brought from Washington, D.C.,
And spread among such friends as might occur
Of like views with "The Noted Traveler."

The Hired Man's Dog-Story

Twa dogs that were na thrang at hame
Forgather'd ance upon a time.
—BURNS.

Dogs, I contend, is jes' about
Nigh human — git 'em studied out.
I hold, like us, they've got their own
Reasonin' powers 'at's theirs alone —
Same as their tricks and habits too,
Provin', by lots o' things they do,
That instinct's not the only thing
That dogs is governed by, i jing! —
And I'll say furder, on that line,
  And prove it, that they's dogs a-plenty
Will show intelligence as fine
  As ary ten men out o' twenty!

Jevver investigate the way
Sheep-killin' dogs goes at it—hey?
Well, you dig up the facts and you
Will find, first thing, they's always *two*
Dogs goes together on that spree
O' blood and puore dog-deviltry!
And, then, they always go at night—
Mind ye, it's never in daylight,
When folks is up and wide awake,—
No self-respectin' dogs'll make
Mistakes o' judgment on that score,—
And I've knowed fifty head or more
O' slaughtered sheep found in the lot,
Next morning the old farmer got
His folks up and went out to feed,—
And every livin' soul agreed
That all night long they never heerd
The bark o' dog ner bleat o' skeered
And racin', tromplin' flock o' sheep
  A-skallyhootin' roun' the pastur',
To rouse 'em from their peaceful sleep
  To that heart-renderin' disaster!

Well, now, they's actchul evidence
In all these facts set forth; and hence
When, by like facts, it has been foun'
That these two dogs—colloguin' roun'
At night as thick as thieves—*by day*
Don't go together anyway,
And, 'pearantly, hain't never met
Each other; and the facts is set
On record furder, that these smart
Old pards in crime lives miles apart—
Which is a trick o' theirs, to throw
Off all suspicion, don't you know!—
One's a *town*-dog—belongin' to
Some good man, maybe—er to you!—
And one's a *country*-dog, er "*jay*,"
As you nickname us thataway.
Well, now!—these is the facts I' got

(And, mind ye, these *is* facts—not *guesses*)
To argy on, concernin' what
Fine reasonin' powers dogs p'sesses.

My idy is,—the dog lives in
The *town*, we'll say, runs up ag'in
The *country*-dog, some Saturday,
Under a' old farm-wagon, say,
Down at the Court-house hitchin'-rack.—
Both lifts the bristles on their back
And show their teeth and growl as though
They meant it pleasant-like and low,
In case the fight hangs fire. And they
Both wag then in a friendly way,
The town-dog sayin':—"Seems to me,
Last Dimocratic jubilee,
I seen you here in town somewhere?"
The country-dog says:—"Right you air!—
And right here's where you seen me, too,
Under this wagon, watchin' *you!*"
"Yes," says the town-dog,—"and I thought
We'd *both* bear watchin', like as not."
And as he yawns and looks away,
The country-dog says, "What's your lay?"
The town-dog whets his feet a spell
And yawns ag'in, and then says,—"Well,
Before I answer that—Ain't you
A Mill Crick dog, a mile er two
From old Chape Clayton's stock-farm—say?"
"Who *told* you?" says the jay-dog—"hey?"
And looks up, real su'prised. "*I guessed*,"
The town-dog says—"*You* tell the rest,—
How's old Chape's mutton, anyhow?—
How many of 'em's ready now—
How many of 'em's ripe enough fer use,
And how's the hot, red, rosy juice?"
" 'Mm!" says the country-dog, "I think
I sort o' see a little blink
O' what you mean." And then he stops
And turns and looks up street and lops

His old wet tongue out, and says he,
Lickin' his lips, all slobbery,
"Ad-drat my melts! you're jes' my man!—
I'll trust you, 'cause I know I can!"
And then he says, "I'll tell you jes'
How things is, and Chape's carelessness
About his sheep,—fer instance, say,
To-morry Chapes'll all be 'way
To Sund'y-meetin'—and ag'in
At night." "At night? That lets us in!—
'Better the day' "—the town-dog says—
" 'Better the deed.' We'll pray; Lord, yes!—
May the outpourin' grace be shed
Abroad, and all hearts comforted
Accordin' to their lights!" says he,
"And that, of course, means you and me."
And then they both snarled, low and quiet—
Swore where they'd meet. And both stood by it!
Jes' half-past eight on Sund'y night,
Them two dogs meets,—the *town*-dog, light
O' foot, though five mile' he had spanned
O' field, beech-wood and bottom-land.
But, as books says,—we draw a veil
Over this chapter of the tale! . . .
Yit when them two infernal, mean,
Low, orn'ry whelps has left the scene
O' carnage—chased and putt to death
The last pore sheep,—they've yit got breath
Enough to laugh and joke about
The fun they've had, while they sneak out
The woods-way fer the old crick where
They both plunge in and wash their hair
And rench their bloody mouths, and grin,
As each one skulks off home ag'in—
Jes' innardly too proud and glad
  To keep theirselves from kind o' struttin',
Thinkin' about the fun they'd had—
  When their blame wizzens needed cuttin'!

Dogs is deliber't.—They can bide

Their time till s'picions all has died.
The country-dog don't 'pear to care
Fer town no more,—he's off somewhere
When the folks whistles, as they head
The team t'ards town. As I jes' said,—
Dogs is deliber't, don't forgit!
So this-here dog he's got the grit
To jes' deprive hisse'f o' town
For 'bout three weeks. But time rolls roun'! . . .
Same as they *first* met:—Saturday—
Same Court-house—hitch-rack—and same way
The team wuz hitched—same wagon where
The same *jay*-dog growls under there
When same *town*-dog comes loafin' by,
With the most innocentest eye
And giner'l meek and lowly style,
As though he'd never cracked a smile
In all his mortal days!—And both
Them dogs is strangers, you'd take oath!—
  Both keeps a-lookin' sharp, to see
If folks is watchin'—jes' the way
They acted that first Saturday
  They talked so confidentchully.
"Well"—says the town-dog, in a low
And careless tone—"Well, whatch you know?"
" '*Know?*' " says the country-dog—"Lots more
Than some smart people knows—that's shore!"
And then, in his dog-language, he
Explains how slick he had to be
When some suspicious folks come roun'
A-tryin' to track and run him down—
  Like *he'd* had anything to do
With killin' over fifty head
O' sheep! "Jes' think!—and *me*"—he said,
  "And me as innocent as *you*,
That very hour, five mile' away
In this town like you air to-day!"
"Ah!" says the town-dog, "there's the beauty
  O' bein' *prepared* for what may be,
And *washin'* when you've done your duty!—

No stain o' blood on you er me
Ner wool in *our* teeth!—*Then*," says he,
"When wicked man has wronged us so,
We ort to learn to be forgivin'—
Half the world, of course, don't know
How the other gits its livin'!"

His Pa's Romance

All 'at I ever want to be
Is ist to be a man like Pa
When he wuz young an' married Ma!
Uncle he telled us yisterdy
Ist all about it then—'cause they,
My Pa an' Ma, wuz bofe away
To 'tend P'tracted Meetin', where
My Pa an' Ma is allus there
When all the big "Revivals" is,
An' "Love-Feasts," too, an' "Class," an' "Prayer,"
An' when's "Comoonian Servicis."
An', yes, an' Uncle said to not
To never tell *them* ner let on
Like we knowed now ist how they got
First married. So—while they wuz gone—
Uncle he telled us ever'thing—
'Bout how my Pa wuz ist a pore
Farm-boy.—He says, I tell you *what*,
Your Pa *wuz* pore! But neighbers they
All liked him—all but one old man
An' his old wife that folks all say
Nobody liked, ner never can!
Yes, sir! an' Uncle purt' nigh swore
About the mean old man an' way
He treat' my Pa!—'cause he's a pore
Farm-hand—but prouder 'an a king—
An' ist work' on, he did, an' wore
His old patched clo'es, ist anyway,
So he saved up his wages—then
He ist worked on an' saved some more,

An' ist worked on, ist night an' day—
Till, sir, he save' up nine er ten
Er hunnerd dollars! But he keep
All still about it, Uncle say—
But he ist thinks—an' thinks a heap!
Though what he wuz a-thinkin', Pa
He never tell' a soul but Ma—
(Then, course, you know, he wuzn't Pa,
An', course, you know, she wuzn't Ma—
They wuz ist sweethearts, course you know);
'Cause Ma wuz ist a girl, about
Sixteen; an' when my Pa he go
A-courtin' her, her Pa an' Ma—
The very first they find it out—
Wuz maddest folks you ever saw!
'Cause it wuz her old Ma an' Pa
'At hate' my Pa, an' toss their head,
An' ist raise Ned! An' her Pa said
He'd ruther see his daughter dead!
An' said she's ist a child!—an' so
Wuz Pa!—An' ef he wuz man-grown
An' only man on earth below,
His daughter shouldn't marry him
Ef he's a king an' on his throne!
Pa's chances then looked mighty slim
Fer certain, Uncle said. But he—
He never told a soul but her
What he wuz keepin' quiet fer.
Her folks ist lived a mile from where
He lived at—an' they drove past there
To git to town. An' ever' one
An' all the neighbers they liked her
An' showed it! But her folks—no, sir!—
Nobody liked her parunts none!
An' so when they shet down, you know,
On Pa—an' old man tell' him so—
Pa ist went back to work, an' she
Ist waited. An', sir! purty soon
Her folks they thought he's turned his eye
Some other way—'cause by-an'-by

They heard he'd *rented* the old place
He worked on. An' one afternoon
A neighber, that had bust' a trace,
He tell' the old man they wuz signs
Around the old place that the young
Man wuz a-fixin' up the old
Log cabin some, an' he had brung
New furnichur from town; an' told
How th' old house 'uz whitewashed clean
An' sweet wiv morning-glory vines
An' hollyhawks all 'round the door
An' winders—an' a bran'-new floor
In th' old porch—an' wite-new green-
An'-red pump in the old sweep-well!

An', Uncle said, when he hear tell
O' all them things, the old man he
Ist grin' an' says, he "reckon' now
Some gal, er widder anyhow,
That silly boy he's coaxed at last
To marry him!" he says, says-ee,
"An' ef he has, 'so mote it be'!"
Then went back to the house to tell
His *wife* the news, as he went past
The smokehouse, an' then went on in
The kitchen, where his daughter she
Wuz washin', to tell *her*, an' grin
An' try to worry her a spell!
The mean old thing! But Uncle said
She ain't cry much—ist pull her old
Sunbonnet forrerds on her head—
So's old man he can't see her face
At all! An' when he s'pose he scold
An' jaw enough, he ist clear' out
An' think he's boss of all the place!

Then Uncle say, the first you know
They's go' to be a Circus-show
In town; an' old man think he'll take
His wife an' go. An' when she say

To take their daughter, too, *she* shake
Her head like she don't *want* to go;
An' when he sees she wants to stay,
The old man takes her, anyway!
An' so she went! But Uncle he
Said she looked mighty sweet that day,
Though she wuz pale as she could be,
A-speshully a-drivin' by
Wite where her beau lived at, you know;
But out the corner of his eye
The old man watch' her; but she throw
Her pairsol 'round so she can't see
The house at all! An' then she hear
Her Pa an' Ma a-talkin' low
An' kind o' laughin'-like; but she
Ist set there in the seat behind,
P'tendin' like she didn't mind.
An', Uncle say, when they got past
The young man's place, an' 'pearantly
He wuzn't home, but off an' gone
To town, the old man turned at last
An' talked back to his daughter there,
All pleasant-like, from then clean on
Till they got into town, an' where
The Circus wuz, an' on inside
O' that, an' through the crowd, on to
The very top seat in the tent
Wite next the band—a-bangin' through
A tune 'at bu'st his yeers in two!
An' there the old man scrouged an' tried
To make his wife set down, an' she
A-yellin'! But ist what she meant
He couldn't hear, ner couldn't see
Till she turned 'round an' pinted. Then
He turned an' looked—an' looked again! . . .
He ist saw neighbers ever'where—
But, sir, *his daughter* wuzn't there!
An', Uncle says, he even saw
Her beau, you know, he hated so;
An' he wuz with some other girl.

An' then he heard the Clown "Haw-haw!"
An' saw the horses wheel an' whirl
Around the ring, an' heard the zipp
O' the Ringmaster's long slim whip—
But that whole Circus, Uncle said,
Wuz all inside the old man's head!

An' Uncle said, he didn't find
His daughter all that afternoon—
An' her Ma says she'll lose her mind
Ef they don't find her purty soon!
But, though they looked all day, an' stayed
There fer the night p'formance—not
No use at all!—they never laid
Their eyes on her. An' then they got
Their team out, an' the old man shook
His fist at all the town, an' then
Shook it up at the moon ag'in,
An' said his time 'ud come, some day!
An' jerked the lines an' driv away.

Uncle, he said, he s'pect, that night,
The old man's madder yet when they
Drive past the young man's place, an' hear
A fiddle there, an' see a light
Inside, an' shadders light an' gay
A-dancin' 'crosst the winder-blinds.
An' some young chaps outside yelled, "Say!
What 'pears to be the hurry—hey?"
But the old man ist whipped the lines
An' streaked past like a runaway!
An' now you'll be su'prised, I bet!—
I hardly ain't quit laughin' yet
When Uncle say, that jamboree
An' dance an' all—w'y, that's a sign
That any old man ort to see,
As plain as 8 and 1 makes 9,
That they's *a weddin'* wite inside
That very house he's whippin' so
To git apast!—An', sir! the bride

There's his own daughter! Yes, an' oh!
She's my Ma now—an' young man she
Got married, he's my Pa! *Whoop-ee!*
But Uncle say to not laugh all
The laughin' yet, but please save some
To kind o' spice up what's to come!

Then Uncle say, about next day
The neighbers they begin to call
An' wish 'em well, an' say how glad
An' proud an' tickled ever' way
Their friends all is—an' how they had
The lovin' prayers of ever' one
That had homes of their own! But none
Said nothin' 'bout the home that she
Had run away from! So she sighed
Sometimes—an' wunst she purt' nigh cried.

Well, Uncle say, her old Pa, he
Ist like to died, he wuz so mad!
An' her Ma, too! But by-an'-by
They cool down some.
An', 'bout a week,
She want to see her Ma so bad,
She think she'll haf to go! An' so
She coax him; an' he kiss her cheek
An' say, Lord bless her, *course* they'll go!
An', Uncle say, when they're bofe come
A-knockin' there at her old home—
W'y, first he know, the door it flew
Open, all quick, an' she's jerked in,
An', quicker still, the door's banged to
An' locked: an' crosst the winder-sill
The old man pokes a shotgun through
An' says to git! "You stold my child,"
He says: "an', now she's back, w'y, you
Clear out, this minute, er I'll kill
You! Yes, an' I 'ull kill her, too,
Ef you don't go!" An' then, all wild,
His young wife begs him please to go!

An' so he turn' an' walk'—all slow
An' pale as death, but awful still
An' ca'm—back to the gate, an' on
Into the road, where he had gone
So many times alone, you know!
An', Uncle say, a whipperwill
Holler so lonesome, as he go
On back to'rds home, he say he 'spec'
He ist 'ud like to wring its neck!
An' I ain't think he's goin' back
All by hisse'f—but Uncle say
That's what he does, an' it's a fac'!
An' 'pears-like he's goin' back to *stay*—
'Cause there he stick', ist thataway,
An' don't go nowheres any more,
Ner don't nobody ever see
Him set his foot outside the door—
Till 'bout five days, a boy loped down
The road, a-comin' past from town,
An' he called to him from the gate,
An' sent the old man word: He's thought
Things over now; an', while he hate
To lose his wife, he think she ought
To mind her Pa an' Ma an' do
Whatever *they* advise her to.
An' sends word, too, to come an' git
Her new things an' the furnichur
That he had special' bought fer her—
'Cause, now that they wuz goin' to quit,
She's free to ist have all of it;—
So, fer his love fer her, he say
To come an' git it, wite away.
An' *spang!* that very afternoon,
Here come her Ma—ist 'bout as soon
As old man could hitch up an' tell
Her "hurry back!" An' 'bout as quick
As she's drove there to where my Pa—
I mean to where her son-in-law—
Lives at, he meets her at the door
All smilin', though he's awful pale

An' trimbly—like he's ist been sick;
He take her in the house—An', 'fore
She knows it, they's a cellar-door
Shet on her, an' she hears the click
Of a' old rusty padlock! Then,
Uncle, he say, she kind o' stands
An' thinks—an' thinks—an' thinks ag'in—
An' mayby thinks of her own child
Locked up—like her! An' Uncle smiled,
An' I ist laughed an' clapped my hands!
An' there she stayed! An' she can cry
Ist all she want! an' yell an' kick
To ist her heart's content! an' try
To pry out wiv a quiltin'-stick!
But Uncle say he guess at last
She's 'bout give up, an' holler through
The door-crack fer to please to be
So kind an' good as send an' tell
The old man, like she want him to,
To come 'fore night, an' set her free,
Er—they wuz rats down there! An' yell
She did, till, Uncle say, it soured
The morning's milk in the back yard!
But all the answer reached her, where
She's skeered so in the dark down there,
Wuz ist a mutterin' that she heard,—
"I've sent him word!—I've sent him word!"
An' shore enough, as Uncle say,
He *has* "sent word!"

Well, it's plum night
An' all the house is shet up tight—
Only one winder 'bout half-way
Raised up, you know; an' ain't no light
Inside the whole house, Uncle say.
Then, first you know, there where the team
Stands hitched yet, there the old man stands—
A' old tin lantern in his hands
An' monkey-wrench; an' he don't seem
To make things out, a-standin' there.

He comes on to the gate an' feels
An' fumbles fer the latch—then hears
A voice that chills him to the heels—
"You halt! an' stand right where you air!"
Then, sir! my—my—his son-in-law,
There at the winder wiv his gun,
He tell the old man what he's done:
"You hold *my* wife a prisoner—
An' *your* wife, drat ye! I've got *her!*
An' now, sir," Uncle say he say,
"You ist turn round an' climb wite in
That wagon, an' drive home ag'in
An' bring my wife back wite away,
An' we'll trade then—an' not before
Will I unlock my cellar-door—
Not fer your wife's sake ner your own,
But *my* wife's sake—an' hers alone!"
An', Uncle say, it don't sound like
It's so, but yet it is!—He say,
From wite then, somepin' seem' to strike
The old man's funny-bone some way;
An', minute more, that team o' his
Went tearin' down the road *k'whiz!*
An' in the same two-forty style
Come whizzin' back! An' oh, that-air
Sweet girl a-cryin' all the while,
Thinkin' about her Ma there, shet
In her own daughter's cellar, where—
Ist week or so *she's* kep' house there—
She hadn't time to clean it yet!
So when her Pa an' her they git
There—an' the young man grab' an' kiss
An' hug her, till she make him quit
An' ask him where her mother is.
An' then he smile' an' try to not;
Then slow-like find th' old padlock key,
An' blow a' oat-hull out of it,
An' then stoop down there where he's got
Her Ma locked up so keerfully—
An' where, wite there, he say he thought

It *ort* to been *the old man*—though
Uncle, he say, he reckon not—
When out she bounced, all tickled so
To taste fresh air ag'in an' find
Her folks wunst more, an' grab' her child
An' cry an' laugh, an' even go
An' hug the old man; an' he wind
Her in his arms, an' laugh, an' pat
Her back, an' say he's riconciled,
In such a happy scene as that,
To swap his daughter for her Ma,
An' have so smart a son-in-law
As *they* had! "Yes, an' he's my Pa!"
I laugh' an' yell', "Hooray-hooraw!"

A Backward Look

As I sat smoking, alone, yesterday,
  And lazily leaning back in my chair,
Enjoying myself in a general way—
Allowing my thoughts a holiday
  From weariness, toil and care,—
My fancies—doubtless, for ventilation—
  Left ajar the gates of my mind,—
And Memory, seeing the situation,
  Slipped out in the street of "Auld Lang Syne."—

Wandering ever with tireless feet
  Through scenes of silence, and jubilee
Of long-hushed voices; and faces sweet
Were thronging the shadowy side of the street
  As far as the eye could see;
Dreaming again, in anticipation,
  The same old dreams of our boyhood's days
That never come true, from the vague sensation
  Of walking asleep in the world's strange ways.

Away to the house where I was born!
  And there was the selfsame clock that ticked

From the close of dusk to the burst of morn,
When life-warm hands plucked the golden corn
  And helped when the apples were picked.
And the "chany dog" on the mantel-shelf,
  With the gilded collar and yellow eyes,
Looked just as at first, when I hugged myself
  Sound asleep with the dear surprise.

And down to the swing in the locust-tree,
  Where the grass was worn from the trampled ground,
And where "Eck" Skinner, "Old" Carr, and three
Or four such other boys used to be
  "Doin' sky-scrapers," or "whirlin' round":
And again Bob climbed for the blue-bird's nest,
  And again "had shows" in the buggy-shed
Of Guymon's barn, where still, unguessed,
  The old ghosts romp through the best days dead!

And again I gazed from the old schoolroom
  With a wistful look, of a long June day,
When on my cheek was the hectic bloom
Caught of Mischief, as I presume—
  He had such a "partial" way,
It seemed, toward me.—And again I thought
  Of a probable likelihood to be
Kept in after school—for a girl was caught
  Catching a note from me.

And down through the woods to the swimming-hole—
  Where the big, white, hollow old sycamore grows,—
And we never cared when the water was cold,
And always "ducked" the boy that told
  On the fellow that tied the clothes.—
When life went so like a dreamy rhyme,
  That it seems to me now that then
The world was having a jollier time
  Than it ever will have again.

What Smith Knew About Farming

There wasn't two purtier farms in the state
Than the couple of which I'm about to relate;—
Jinin' each other—belongin' to Brown,
And jest at the edge of a flourishin' town.
Brown was a man, as I understand,
That allus had handled a good 'eal o' land,
And was sharp as a tack in drivin' a trade—
For that's the way most of his money was made.
And all the grounds and the orchards about
His two pet farms was all tricked out
With poppies and posies
And sweet-smellin' rosies;
And hundreds o' kinds
Of all sorts o' vines,
To tickle the most horticultural minds;
And little dwarf trees not as thick as your wrist
With ripe apples on 'em as big as your fist:
And peaches—Siberian crabs and pears,
And quinces—Well! *any* fruit *any* tree bears;
And the purtiest stream—jest a-swimmin' with fish
And—*jest a'most everything heart could wish!*
The purtiest orch'rds—I wish you could see
How purty they was, fer I know it 'ud be
A regular treat!—but I'll go ahead with
My story! A man by the name o' Smith—
(A bad name to rhyme,
But I reckon that I'm
Not goin' back on a Smith! nary time!)
'At hadn't a soul of kin nor kith,
And more money than he knowed what to do with,—
So he comes a-ridin' along one day,
And *he* says to Brown, in his offhand way—
Who was trainin' some newfangled vines round a bay-
Winder—"Howdy-do—look-a-here—say:
What'll you take fer this property here?—
I'm talkin' o' leavin' the city this year,

And I want to be
Where the air is free,
And I'll *buy* this place, if it ain't too dear!"—
Well—they grumbled and jawed aroun'—
"I don't like to part with the place," says Brown;
"Well," says Smith, a-jerkin' his head,
"That house yonder—bricks painted red—
Jest like this'n—a *purtier view*—
Who is it owns *it*?" "That's mine too,"
Says Brown, as he winked at a hole in his shoe,
"But I'll tell you right here jest what I *kin* do:—
If you'll pay the figgers I'll sell *it* to you."
Smith went over and looked at the place—
Badgered with Brown, and argied the case—
Thought that Brown's figgers was rather too tall,
But, findin' that Brown wasn't goin' to fall,
In final agreed,
So they drawed up the deed
Fer the farm and the fixtures—the live stock an' all.
And so Smith moved from the city as soon
As he possibly could—But "the man in the moon"
Knowed more'n Smith o' farmin' pursuits,
And jest to convince you, and have no disputes,
How little he knowed,
I'll tell you his "mode,"
As he called it, o' raisin' "the best that growed,"
In the way o' potatoes—
Cucumbers—tomatoes,
And squashes as lengthy as young alligators.
'Twas allus a curious thing to me
How big a fool a feller kin be
When he gits on a farm after leavin' a town!—
Expectin' to raise himself up to renown,
And reap fer himself agricultural fame,
By growin' of squashes—*without any shame*—
As useless and long as a technical name.
To make the soil pure,
And certainly sure,
He plastered the ground with patent manure.
He had cultivators, and double-hoss plows,

And patent machines fer milkin' his cows;
And patent hay-forks—patent measures and weights,
And new patent back-action hinges fer gates,
And barn locks and latches, and such little dribs,
And patents to keep the rats out o' the cribs—
Reapers and mowers,
And patent grain sowers;
And drillers
And tillers
And cucumber hillers,
And horries;—and had patent rollers and scrapers,
And took about ten agricultural papers.
So you can imagine how matters turned out:
But *Brown* didn't have not a shadder o' doubt
That Smith didn't know what he was about
When he said that "the *old* way to farm was played out."
But Smith worked ahead,
And when any one said
That the *old* way o' workin' was better instead
O' his "modern idees," he allus turned red,
And wanted to know
What made people so
Infernally anxious to hear theirselves crow?
And guessed that he'd manage to hoe his own row.
Brown he come onc't and leant over the fence,
And told Smith that he couldn't see any sense
In goin' to such a tremendous expense
Fer the sake o' such no-account experiments:—
"That'll never make corn!
As shore's you're born
It'll come out the leetlest end of the horn!"
Says Brown, as he pulled off a big roastin'-ear
From a stalk of his own
That had tribble outgrown
Smith's poor yaller shoots, and says he, "Looky here!
This corn was raised in the old-fashioned way,
And I rather imagine that *this* corn'll pay
Expenses fer *raisin'* it!—What do you say?"
Brown got him then to look over his crop.—
His luck that season had been tip-top!

And you may surmise
Smith opened his eyes
And let out a look o' the wildest surprise
When Brown showed him punkins as big as the lies
He was stuffin' him with—about offers he's had
Fer his farm: "I don't want to sell very bad,"
He says, but says he,
"Mr. Smith, you kin see
Fer yourself how matters is standin' with me,
I understand farmin' and I'd better stay,
You know, on my farm;—I'm a-makin' it pay—
I oughtn't to grumble!—I reckon I'll clear
Away over four thousand dollars this year."
And that was the reason, he made it appear,
Why he didn't care about sellin' his farm,
And hinted at his havin' done himself harm
In sellin' the other, and wanted to know
If Smith wouldn't sell back ag'in to him.—So
Smith took the bait, and says he, "Mr. Brown,
I wouldn't *sell* out but we might swap aroun'—
How'll you trade your place fer mine?"
(Purty sharp way o' comin' the shine
Over Smith! Wasn't it?) Well, sir, this Brown
Played out his hand and brought Smithy down—
Traded with him an', workin' it cute,
Raked in two thousand dollars to boot
As slick as a whistle, an' that wasn't all,—
He managed to trade back ag'in the next fall,—
And the next—and the next—as long as Smith stayed
He reaped with his harvests an annual trade.—
Why, I reckon that Brown must 'a' easily made—
On an *average*—nearly two thousand a year—
Together he made over seven thousand—clear.—
Till Mr. Smith found he was losin' his health
In as big a proportion, almost, as his wealth;
So at last he concluded to move back to town,
And sold back his farm to this same Mr. Brown
At very low figgers, by gittin' it down.
Further'n this I have nothin' to say
Than merely advisin' the Smiths fer to stay

In their grocery stores in flourishin' towns
And leave agriculture alone—and the Browns.

A Summer Afternoon

A languid atmosphere, a lazy breeze,
  With labored respiration, moves the wheat
From distant reaches, till the golden seas
  Break in crisp whispers at my feet.

My book, neglected of an idle mind,
  Hides for a moment from the eyes of men;
Or, lightly opened by a critic wind,
  Affrightedly reviews itself again.

Off through the haze that dances in the shine
  The warm sun showers in the open glade,
The forest lies, a silhouette design
  Dimmed through and through with shade.

A dreamy day; and tranquilly I lie
  At anchor from all storms of mental strain;
With absent vision, gazing at the sky,
  "Like one that hears it rain."

The Katydid, so boisterous last night,
  Clinging, inverted, in uneasy poise,
Beneath a wheat-blade, has forgotten quite
  If "Katy *did* or *didn't*" make a noise.

The twitter, sometimes, of a wayward bird
  That checks the song abruptly at the sound,
And mildly, chiding echoes that have stirred,
  Sink into silence, all the more profound.

And drowsily I hear the plaintive strain
  Of some poor dove . . . Why, I can scarcely keep
My heavy eyelids—there it is again—
  "Coo-coo!"—I mustn't—"Coo-coo!" fall asleep!

The Raggedy Man

O! The Raggedy Man! He works fer Pa;
An' he's the goodest man ever you saw!
He comes to our house every day,
An' waters the horses, an' feeds 'em hay;
An' he opens the shed—an' we all ist laugh
When he drives out our little old wobble-ly calf;
An' nen—ef our hired girl says he can—
He milks the cow fer 'Lizabuth Ann.—
  Ain't he a' awful good Raggedy Man?
    Raggedy! Raggedy! Raggedy Man!

W'y, The Raggedy Man—he's ist so good
He splits the kindlin' an' chops the wood;
An' nen he spades in our garden, too,
An' does most things 'at *boys* can't do!—
He clumbed clean up in our big tree
An' shooked a' apple down fer me—
An' nother'n', too, fer 'Lizabuth Ann—
An' nother'n', too, fer The Raggedy Man.—
  Ain't he a' awful kind Raggedy Man?
    Raggedy! Raggedy! Raggedy Man!

An' The Raggedy Man, he knows most rhymes
An' tells 'em, ef I be good, sometimes:
Knows 'bout Giunts, an' Griffuns, an' Elves,
An' the Squidgicum-Squees 'at swallers therselves!
An', wite by the pump in our pasture-lot,
He showed me the hole 'at the Wunks is got,
'At lives 'way deep in the ground, an' can
Turn into me, er 'Lizabuth Ann,
Er Ma er Pa er The Raggedy Man!
  Ain't he a funny old Raggedy Man?
    Raggedy! Raggedy! Raggedy Man!

The Raggedy Man—one time when he
Wuz makin' a little bow-'n'-orry fer me,

Says "When *you're* big like your Pa is,
Air *you* go' to keep a fine store like his—
An' be a rich merchunt—an' wear fine clothes?—
Er what *air* you go' to be, goodness knows!"
An' nen he laughed at 'Lizabuth Ann,
An' I says " 'M go' to be a Raggedy Man!—
  I'm ist go' to be a nice Raggedy Man!"
    Raggedy! Raggedy! Raggedy Man!

Alphabetical List of Titles

Alphabetical List of First Lines